VEGGIE & VEGAN LONDON

A guide to ethical eating
in the capital

Edward Prendeville

Punk Pasta, see p.17

VEGGIE & VEGAN LONDON

A guide to ethical eating
in the capital

Edward Prendeville

ACKNOWLEDGEMENTS

I'd like to thank everyone at Metro Publications for their help and support in writing this book. Susi Koch and Andrew Kershman were there every step of the way, from designing its pages to providing support and guidance. Andrew also took on the Herculean task of doing all the photography; his images have helped bring the book to life. Lesley Gilmour deserves special mention; her expertly made maps have transformed my ramble of restaurants and shops into a user-friendly, area-coded guide. Our editor, Eve Kershman, has gone to a lot of trouble to save you, the reader, from tripping up over spelling mistakes and wayward grammar, and has turned the book into a far smoother read.

In the year it's taken to research and write this book, I have had the pleasure of visiting a great many vegan and vegetarian restaurants to taste and test what our capital's ethical kitchens are creating. Running an eatery is a difficult enterprise and it has been a joy to meet the chefs, taste their food and hear their stories. Lastly, my thanks go to all the veggies and vegans I have met on my travels whose generous support and recommendations have helped to make this book as comprehensive as it possibly can be.

SMOKED TOFU
SRIRACHA MAYO
TOMATO, HUMMUS
& LEAVES

Contents

South

East

Jam Delish, see p.127

INTRODUCTION

In the years since the first edition of the book, perceptions of veganism have changed almost immeasurably in the public consciousness. It's moved from a fringe movement to a lifestyle habit that a sizable number of us are adopting, whether as hardcore animal activists or flexitarians trying to do their bit for the environment. Despite COVID-19 being the last orders for more than a few establishments covered in the original guide, the majority have bounced back better than ever. What's more, the number of new eateries to emerge, led by innovative young chefs and entrepreneurs, has cemented the place of plant-based dishes on our menus, whether that's with fast-food or fine-dining.

London is easily the vegan capital of the world. From its humble origins in the old-school vegetarian restaurants, like Mildred's and The Gate, to the youth-oriented influx of faux meat street food joints like Temple of Seitan and Halo Burger. There's also a wealth of Middle Eastern, south Asian and Caribbean restaurants like Bubala, Rasa and Jam Delish. It's been a pleasure seeing plant-based cooking make its breakthrough into the world of fine-dining, with the likes of Gauthier showing that it's not about giving anything up, but gaining so much more. But best of all are those local gems: independents and family-run businesses like The Fields Beneath and Persepolis that continue to give character to their neighbourhoods.

All of this and more has been mapped out by area, making exploring both your own backyard and uncharted territory all the easier and more enjoyable. And there are more than just restaurants to check out – these days you can find clothes, household items and groceries from first-rate, sustainable and cruelty-free providers. You won't want to miss these on your travels, but with this book as your guide, there's no excuse not to live a little more vegetarian and vegan in London.

Edward Prendeville

The Spread Eagle, see p.280

RESTAURANTS, CAFÉS & BARS

Plates, see p.266

CENTRAL

BLOOMSBURY & FITZROVIA

1. Flower Burger
2. Kin Café
3. MOMO's Garden Café
4. Namaste Holborn
5. Punk Pasta
6. Sagar
7. Thenga Café
8. Vantra Eden
9. Vetomeato

Shops:

A) Alara Health Store, p.322
B) Planet Organic, Tottenham Court Road p.327

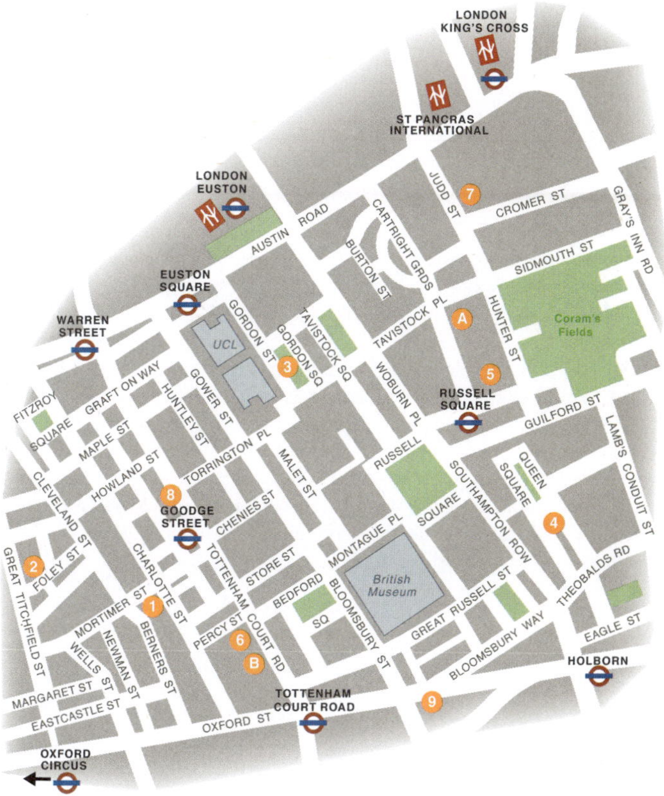
LONDON KING'S CROSS
ST PANCRAS INTERNATIONAL
LONDON EUSTON
EUSTON SQUARE
WARREN STREET
RUSSELL SQUARE
GOODGE STREET
TOTTENHAM COURT ROAD
HOLBORN
OXFORD CIRCUS
UCL
British Museum
Coram's Fields
JUDD ST
CROMER ST
GRAY'S INN RD
SIDMOUTH ST
AUSTIN ROAD
CARTRIGHT GRDS
BURTON ST
TAVISTOCK PL
HUNTER ST
GORDON ST
GORDON SQ
TAVISTOCK SQ
WOBURN PL
GUILFORD ST
LAMB'S CONDUIT ST
FITZROY SQUARE
GRAFT ON WAY
HUNTLEY ST
GOWER ST
MAPLE ST
TORRINGTON PL
MALET ST
RUSSELL SQUARE
SOUTHAMPTON ROW
QUEEN SQUARE
HOWLAND ST
CLEVELAND ST
CHENIES ST
MONTAGUE PL
THEOBALDS RD
GREAT TITCHFIELD ST
FOLEY ST
CHARLOTTE ST
TOTTENHAM COURT RD
STORE ST
BEDFORD SQ
BLOOMSBURY ST
GREAT RUSSELL ST
BLOOMSBURY WAY
EAGLE ST
MORTIMER ST
WELLS ST
NEWMAN ST
BERNERS ST
PERCY ST
MARGARET ST
EASTCASTLE ST
OXFORD ST
1
2
3
4
5
6
7
8
9
A
B

Flower Burger ❶

Technicolour temptations
43 Charlotte Street, W1T 1RS
020 7323 9523
www.flowerburger.co.uk
Insta: @flowerburger_uk
Travel: Goodge Street LU
Sun-Thur 12:00-22:00, Fri-Sat 12:00-23:00

Vegan food is known for being colourful, but I doubt there's anywhere in London with an offering quite like Flower Burger. In the heart of Fitzrovia, you'll find purple, pink and baby blue buns adorning bean patties buried under vibrant salads. There are a handful of sides and desserts on offer, like potato wedges and 'flower bombs' – bite-sized balls of breaded seitan. It's got the same casual setup as a burger chain, with a diner interior and some alfresco seating too. Their combo meals cost around £14, making it price-competitive with similar central London eateries. The psychedelic flower power theme runs through to their ethical origins, as a business that is committed to making plant-based eating more attractive and fun.

££
Vegan

deliveroo
HappyCow
RECOMMENDED
REVIEWED

Kin Café ❷

Family-run café classics
22 Foley Street, W1W 6DT
020 3589 5185
www.kincafe.co.uk
Insta: @kin_cafe
Travel: Goodge Street LU
Mon-Fri 08:30-16:30, Sat-Sun 09:30-16:30

Kin stands out as an oasis of meat-free dining among a host of popular eateries in the backstreets of Bloomsbury. It manages to balance being a friendly, family-run enterprise with loyal regulars, while boasting a trendy, sleek interior that is worthy of a special weekend veggie or vegan breakfast or lunch trip.

They do things a little differently here with their all-day menu, meaning you can eat your favourite brunch foods all day from 8:30 to 14:30 (not just on Sundays). Dishes include their famous burrito stuffed with sweet potato, refried beans and tofu scramble, as well as their stacked fry-ups which come complete with hash browns. Their menu is seasonal, so you'll find something new every time you visit.

The food and drink here are prepared with care, using delicious and healthy produce, so it really doesn't matter if you're popping in for a coffee or lining up to chow down on their weekend brunch specials, you're bound to enjoy the experience. There is indoor and outdoor seating, making this eatery equally suitable for visits on fine days. All-day meals on average cost £15, but expect to leave very full and lighter options like granola will set you back £9. Kin gets no bad marks from us – it's a 5-star veggie and vegan spot.

££
Vegetarian

Organic Coffee
Homemade Cakes & Sandwiches
Vegan Choices

Momo's Garden Café ③

Much-loved garden kiosk in Gordon Square

Gordon Square, WC1H 0PD
Insta: @momosgardencafe
Travel: Euston Square LU
Mon-Fri 08.30-16:00, Sat-Sun 10:00-16:00

Nestled among the trees in tranquil Gordon Square, Momo's kiosk serves healthy and homely vegetarian and vegan food, best enjoyed sitting at their tables or the many surrounding benches. Whether cooling down with an ice cream in the summer heat, recharging overlooking the autumn leaves with a chai latte or tucking into a festive linzer heart in the snow, it's the perfect base from which to enjoy this beautiful green space in any season.

Some may know this as the erstwhile Ginger Jules's, but the new owner, Monika, continues the legacy of great plant-based food. Everything is made on-site, from the salads to the curries and freshly baked cakes. Monika even finds time to create some classic dishes from her native Austria, such as kipferl and käsespätzle – the latter is akin to mac n' cheese. Not only is much of the food on offer vegan (and all vegetarian), but it's also the best value to be found in the area, with cakes, snacks and drinks costing £2 or less, and hot meals for between £3 and £4. In keeping with Momo's eco-principles, discounts apply for anyone with their own mug or cup, and their containers are biodegradable and disposed of in a composter, to be turned into soil for the plants growing around the site. Momo's is one of the best alfresco dining experiences in London, it's certainly a respite from the anonymous corporate cafés that now populate many London parks.

£
Vegetarian

Namaste Holborn 4

Cruelty-free curries
33 Boswell Street, WC1N 3BP
020 8127 1680
www.namasteholborn.com
Insta: @namaste_holborn
Travel: Holborn LU
Mon-Sat 11:30-22:00, Sun 12:00-22:00

Central London isn't exactly in short supply of somewhere to source a curry, but despite the colonial ties between the subcontinent's cuisine and our city, not to mention how most Hindus are vegetarian, finding meat-free fare can be a little more difficult. Fear not though, for the arrival of Namaste Holborn has partially rectified this want, with their thali (platter of curries served in a steel tray) being the first port of call for any hungry travellers in the area. Other highlights include their Bombay sandwich or vada pav - an upgrade to the chip butty that sees the street food staple transformed through herbs, spices and chutney; mogo - cassava wedges swimming in a sauce that makes this sadly-overlooked vegetable taste deceptively meaty; and royal dahl - slow-cooked buttery black lentils that are as rich as the name implies. Whatever takes your fancy from their menu, wash it down with a choice of imported Indian soft drinks that retain their signature all-sugar, no-sweeteners recipe and taste. Namaste Holborn is still very much a homely affair - expect to eat well for around £15.

£-££
Vegetarian

NEVER MIND
THE GRASS
IS GREENER
WHERE

Punk Pasta 5

Anarchists against animal cruelty
4 Brunswick Centre, WC1N 1AE
020 7278 0888
www.punkpasta.co.uk
Insta: @punkpastauk
Travel: Russell Square LU
Mon-Sat 12:00-22:00

One of the hardest aspects of going vegan is the sheer sacrifice of Italian cuisine. Pasta is a favourite dish and yet so often involves copious accompanying quantities of dairy and meat, not to mention how often it is made using eggs. An anecdote commonly heard is the stunned look on a nonna's face when told their grandchild cannot eat their cooking anymore. But worry no longer. Punk Pasta is London's newest, finest pasta establishment and is 100% vegan. Plant-based takes on maccheroni alle polpette (spaghetti and meatballs), pasta pesto and aglio olio are just some of the classic dishes on offer. With prices around £10 for a plate of pasta, and a bruschetta or panna cotta at either side for around half of that, it's no surprise it has proved an instant success. The space is large and comfortable should you want a more sit-down affair, but still casual enough for a quick bite at the counter. We recommend you give Punk Pasta a try.

£-££
Vegan

Branch

Sagar 6

South Indian
17a Percy Street, W1T 1DU
www.sagarveg.co.uk
Full review see p.53

Thenga Café 7

It's thali time

120 Cromer Street, WC1H 8BS
0788 497 4392
www.thengacafe.com
Insta: @thengacafe
Travel: King's Cross LU
Mon-Thur 11:00-19:00, Fri 11:00-17:00, Sat 11:00-16:00

You could walk past the brick walls of 120 Cromer Street without ever realising what lay behind them, unless you were lucky enough to spot the blackboard outside advertising Thenga Café. Inside, the modest canteen environment of the place doesn't do justice to the special food and service you'll find here. The building itself is split between a yoga studio and the eatery, with the latter offering a good selection of organic hot and cold drinks and vegetarian baked goods throughout the day.

Their speciality, however, is the daily rotating vegan curries, served in the classic steel tray style (where you get a variety of curries alongside rice and usually roti). Thenga will give you a taste of authentic Indian food, a rare find among the proliferation of anglicised Indian restaurants. Expect great service from the friendly staff as you relax for lunch in the café's high-ceilinged and quirkily decorated space. Thenga is popular with the local student community drawn by their great value, daily set meal for just £6.95 and organic coffees, homemade masala chai tea and juices for around £2. Thenga is a great option for a budget vegetarian meal in the capital and one heartily recommended.

£
Vegetarian

World-class
education
equipment.

Vantra Eden 8

Oasis just off Tottenham Court Road

79a Tottenham Court Road, W1T 4TD
07586 350 076
www.vantra.co.uk
Insta: @vantralondon
Travel: Goodge Street LU
Tue-Sat 12:00-16:00, 17:00-22:00

This latest outpost of a long-standing vegan health-food restaurant group provides a welcome oasis from the adjacent bustle of one of the capital's busiest shopping streets. The focus is on raw, fermented and steamed vegetables served alongside hearty stews packed full of pulses and rich in flavour. They also make fruit smoothies to satisfy your thirst and bao buns to binge on should you need that something extra. Options are limited to four different mains, but prices more than compensate - expect to eat very well for under £10. It's a slightly rag-tag affair with minimal, alfresco seating, so this spot is best used as somewhere to grab something to take away. For a more elaborate, sit-down meal you could try their restaurant, Vantra Vegan, in Soho (see p.54).

£
Vegan

Vetomeato 9

Puns meet plant-based
33 New Oxford Street, WC1A 1BH
www.vetomeato.com
Insta: @vetomeato
Travel: Holborn LU
Mon-Fri 12:00-22:00, Sat 12:00-17:00

Located in The Old Crown Public House, this isn't the first time a vegan chef has joined forces with a London pub, but it is one of the few places in the area where you'll be able to pair pints with plant-based grub. They offer a street food-focused selection that ranges from Thai larbs to Turkish kebabs, as well as American burgers and 'Asian bowls' (similar to bibimbap - a Korean dish of rice, kimchi, gochujang and vegetables). With prices around £7, this is a very affordable affair for such a central part of the city, and a good way to dose up on lots of tasty veg, or fake meats galore should you prefer. But what we love most about this place is the story behind it - chef-owner Justin managed to turn around a life on the streets a few years ago into a successful business here and now. So let's put our money where our mouths wander and support this welcome addition to the capital.

£
Vegan

THE CITY

❶ Falafel House
❷ Flipside
❸ Pastan
❹ Pilpel Fleet Street
❺ Pilpel St Paul's
❻ Pilpel Lime Street
❼ Stem & Glory
❽ Whitecross Street Market:
  Village Kitchen
  Buddha Bowl

8
WHITECROSS ST
Bunhill Fields
BARBICAN
3
2
CHISWELL ST
BEECH ST
SILK ST
ROPEMAKER ST
Smithfield Market
ALDERSGATE ST
Barbican
7
MOORGATE
FORE ST
LITTLE BRITAIN
LONDON WALL
LONDON WALL
NEWGATE ST
MOORGATE
WOOD ST
GRESHAM ST
5
ST PAUL'S
LOTHBURY
PATERNOSTER SQ
NEW CHANGE
CHEAPSIDE
THREADNEEDLE ST
KING ST
1
St Paul's
LUDGATE HILL
CARTER LANE
BANK
CORNHILL
QUEEN VICTORIA ST
MANSION HOUSE
LOMBARD ST
GRACECHURCH ST
6
QUEEN VICTORIA ST
CANNON ST
UPPER THAMES ST
MONUMENT
CANNON STREET
MILLENNIUM BRIDGE
SOUTHWARK BRIDGE
Thames Path
Tate Modern
LONDON BRIDGE
STONEY ST

Falafel House ❶

Falafel in the heart of the City

48 Carter Lane, EC4V 5EA
020 7248 3228
www.falafel-house.co.uk
Travel: St Paul's LU
Mon-Fri 11:00-15:00

This easy-going falafel eatery can get very busy during lunch service, as it caters to the vast workforce of the City's financial area. It has a reputation for plentiful portions and perfect pittas and fillings, all for not too much money and easy to eat on the go. A falafel sandwich can be enjoyed for a fiver, and you only need to pay a quid or two extra to load up with some sides like grilled aubergine, feta cheese or guacamole. If you visit with friends you'll be able to eat to your hearts content with their platter for four (£29). There is limited seating, but with no nonsense service and little in the way of décor, Falafel House is ideal for a tasty takeaway lunch that doesn't break the bank.

£
Vegetarian

Flipside ❷

Fast food for the future

88-89 Cowcross Street, EC1M 6BP
020 7250 1103
www.flipsidefood.com
Insta: @flipside_food
Travel: Farringdon LU
Mon-Wed & Fri 08:00-21:00, Thur 08:00-22:00

Despite the recent revolution of plant-based offerings across chain food outlets in the UK, vegan fast food hasn't entirely escaped its lacklustre reputation. But here, to flip that on its head, is a fast-food establishment 'for the future', centrally located in Farringdon, for all comers to enjoy. Flipside serve up a phenomenal range, from cooked breakfasts to salad bowls and burritos, but burgers are perhaps what they do best. Buffalo tenders and Mac n' Cheese are bound to tempt you too, but when breakfast and lunchtime mains cost less than £5, you'll hardly be breaking the bank. The cost roughly doubles at dinner time, which makes sense considering most trade has cleared out of the area with the end of the working day. The arrangement of the space as half-diner, half takeout spot, with a card-only policy and self-service machines available. This gives you the option should you want to grab something on the go or otherwise sit in and relax on their bench Seating. Whatever your preference, be sure to think of Flipside when passing through this part of town.

£
Vegan

Pastan 3

Spagetti for the soul
12-14 St John Street, EC1M 4AY
0798 4979 627
www.pastan.co.uk
Insta: @pastan.uk
Travel: Barbican LU
Tue-Fri 17:00-21:30, Sat 12:00-21:30

St. John Street is famous for its meaty food, not least owing to the centuries-old Smithfield Market next door, so Pastan makes for a change as a 100% vegan addition to the area's eateries. Their adaptations of classic dishes mean you can enjoy home comforts like pasta pomodoro, to classier classics like tortelli di zucca (pumpkin and sage tortellini) without any guilt attached. What's more, the food looks fantastic here.

With a plate of pasta costing around £8 at lunchtime or £15 at dinner, and desserts like gelato or speculoos for less than half that, it's a well-placed competitor to the surrounding businesses, hidden away, as it is, just a stone's throw from the Barbican. The interior is an attractive mix of exposed brick and mid-century furnishings which means pasta is back on the menu for date night. Pastan can also double up if you need of a quick bite to eat when your in the area. A welcome newcomer to Barbican's food scene.

£-££
Vegan

Pilpel

Palate-pleasing Pittas

www.pilpel.co.uk

Insta: @pilpelforthepeople

4 Fleet Street
146 Fleet Street, 1a Wine Office Court, EC4M 3BY
Mon-Fri 11:00-16:00

5 St Paul's
Unit 5, Queen's Head Passage, Paternoster Square, EC4M 7DZ
Mon-Fri 11:00-21:00

6 Lime Street
21 Lime Street, EC3V 1PL
Mon-Fri 11:00-16:00

Pilpel is a 100% vegetarian chain only found within the parameters of the City of London. It has thrived by catering for the large numbers of workers looking for a quick, good-quality lunch. Pilpel takes a no-nonsense approach to falafel and houmous dishes, served fresh from the pan alongside great salads and pittas. There's plenty of seating but during lunch hour it gets busy. The service is remarkably quick even at busy times and they don't mess around with their prices either – £6 for a hearty lunch. Pilpel is a great value eatery and a real gem

£
Vegetarian

Other Branches:

Aldgate, 60 Alie Street, E1 8PX
Old Spitalfields Market, Pavillion Building, E1 6EW
Spitalfields, 38 Brushfield Street, E1 6AT

Stem & Glory 7

Plant-based pedigree
60 Bartholomew Close, EC1A 7BF
020 3990 2034
www.stemandglory.uk
Insta: @stemandglory
Travel: Barbican LU
Tue-Thur 12:00-22:00, Fri & Sat 12:00-23:00

Few plant-based places have the pedigree of high-end restaurants, but Stem & Glory is pushing that boundary. In its short time in operation, it has already picked up numerous accolades, and one look at the food they serve tells you why. Dishes on offer are as different as tacos, ravioli, katsu curry and mushroom cioppino (a fish stew, here minus the fish), but their diversity doesn't come at the price of the taste. Expect food to be as attractive as it is appetising, making this a great date spot should you be looking to impress a prospective vegan partner.

As for the interior – it's a tastefully eclectic affair, with an airiness fit for afternoon lunches but lighting features that allow for more ambient evening meals. And such alchemy has been achieved without being expensive – £15 for mains, £8 for smaller plates and desserts. This means you can eat well here for under £30. Now that they're expanding outwards – with branches in Cambridge and soon-to-be in Broadgate Circle – you'll have no excuse not to.

£££-£££
Vegan

Whitecross Street Market 8

Whitecross Street, EC1Y 8JH
Travel: Barbican LU
Weekday lunchtimes

Village Kitchen

Best fake meat you'll ever eat

Insta: @village_kitchen_food_market

As a rule, we've not included eateries that also serve meat in the book, which is a testimony to just how special this exception is (their meat offering is served in an entirely separate gazebo). The market stall is run by a friendly Kurdish team, who offer the tastiest vegan takeaway I have ever had. They serve the most convincing and tasty fried (seitan) 'chicken' and 'doner' kebab you'll find in London. What's more, it's all paired with delicious, hearty Middle Eastern bean stews and salads, served either in a wrap or with rice. For just £6.50, this is a real Barbican bargain.

£
Vegan

Buddha Bowl

Enlightened eating from a vintage van

Insta: @buddhabowlvan

David and Charlotte have been serving delicious curries, noodles and fragrant broths from their trusty old Citroen van for years and have built up quite a fan base on Whitecross Street. There are lots of flavour options with steamed garden greens, kimchi and halloumi all in the mix, so you can customise your bowl as you like. They are usually here on Thursdays and Fridays when they are always busy serving hungry regulars.

£
Vegetarian

COVENT GARDEN & SOHO

1. Bubala Soho
2. Clean Kitchen
3. Club Mexicana, Kingsley Court
4. Club Mexicana, Seven Dials
5. Gauthier
6. Govinda's
7. Mildred's
8. Neat Burger
9. Sagar
10. Vantra Vegan
11. Veggie Pret

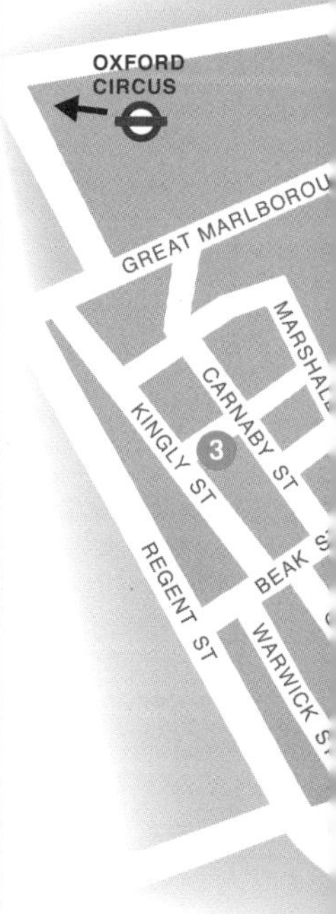

TOTTENHAM
COURT ROAD
OXFORD ST
SOHO
SQUARE
NOEL ST
D'ARBLAY ST
POLAND ST
DEAN ST
FRITH ST
GREEK ST
MANETTE ST
CHARING CROSS RD.
WARDOUR ST
BRIDGE ST
BROADWICK ST
LEXINGTON ST
PETER ST
OLD COMPTON ST
ROMILLY ST
BRIDLE LANE
BREWER ST
SHAFTESBURY AVENUE
GERARD ST
LISLE ST
LEICESTER
SQUARE
DENMAN ST
GLASSHOUSE ST
COVENTRY ST
LEICESTER
SQUARE
HAY MARKET
PANTON ST
PICCADILLY
CIRCUS
1
2
4
5
6
7
8
9
10
11

Bubala Soho ❶

The second branch of a Spitalfields favourite

15 Poland Street, W1F 8QE
www.bubala.co.uk
Insta: @bubala_london
Travel: Oxford Circus LU
Mon-Sat 12:00-15:00 & 17:30-23:00

The renowned Bubala made a reputation for themselves in Spitalfields (see p.294) and have now opened this second branch in the heart of Soho. Bubala is a darling of the vegetarian dining world and this new kitchen is sure to win over any ardent carnivores. The approach is a rejection of the faux-meat side of things in favour of first-class cooking of fresh whole foods. Start things off with some challah and baba ghanoush, before enjoying their sticky corn ribs and camomile and honey-glazed halloumi and onto braised hispi cabbage and confit potato latkes. If you have room, round things off with the date and tahini ice cream and coconut fudge, for there is no such thing as buyer's remorse at Bubala. Their 'We Know Best' feasting menu is also a firm favourite. Dishes range between £3.50 and £15, with most squarely in the middle, so do the sensible thing, and take your family and friends down to enjoy a range of dishes. You could also try the £40 set menu, which takes away the trouble of choosing and gives you a real flavour of this delicious cuisine. And we've not even mentioned the stunningly decorated Soho townhouse that Bubala calls home, where the rustic-chic interior is a respite from the increasingly cookie-cutter restaurants elsewhere in Soho.

££
Vegetarian

Clean Kitchen 2

Junk food but cleaned up

64 Old Compton Street, W1D 4UQ
020 3089 8330
www.cleankitchen.club
Insta: @cleankitchenuk
Travel: Camden Town LU
Mon-Wed 11:00-18:00, Thur-Sun 10:00-20:00

Clean Kitchen are a vegan chain that are expanding rapidly and now have branches across London. Their menu takes a tour of the staples of a plant-based menu - smoothies, acai and salad bowls, burgers and basically as much faux meat as you can eat between two pieces of bread. This is fast food and their stated aim is to become the 'plant-based McDonald's' - so expect all manner of fries, nuggets and desserts like cheesecake too. But as their name suggests, cleanliness is part of the plan; from the sustainability of their ingredients to the use of biodegradable packaging. In truth, it might be a while until they dethrone the cheapest of fast-food chains, with all their burgers costing close to £10. But then again, you don't get luxuries like truffle mayo or smoked 'salmon' at your standard McDonald's, so stop by and see for yourself.

£-££
Vegan

Branches:
126 New Kings Road, SW6 4L
172 Portobello Road, W11 2EB
Boxpark Wembley, Wembley Park, HA9 0JT

Club Mexicana

Club Mexicana 3

Mexican goes meat-free
Kingly Court, W1B 5PW
www.clubmexicana.com
Insta: @clubmexicana
Travel: Piccadilly Circus LU
Mon-Sat 12:00-22:00, Sun 12:00-21:00

Fast becoming one of the key players in London's vegan scene, Club Mexicana was but a pub kitchen pop-up in the first edition of this guide. Now, with its own store in one of the most ideal locations in London, plus a sister site a stone's throw away in Seven Dials, it's surely here to stay. Mexican cuisine has a meaty reputation, but here you can get your taco fix with only plants in the mix. Al pastor (the Mexican pork equivalent of lamb shawarma), baja tofish (a play on the popular cod tacos found along Mexico's coastline) and BBQ 'beef' short rib tacos are just some of what's on offer, all for as little as £4 or 3 for £10. If you're really hungry we recommend the burrito wraps that are stuffed to the brim with nutritious and delicious goodness with the option to add in their 'Holy Guacamole' or refried beans. If you're on a gluten free diet you can swap out the rice with lettuce. Promotions like 'All You Can Eat Taco Tuesdays' make this even better for an early weekday evening sojourn. Kingly Court, where the restaurant resides, has a great alfresco space, making this ideal, come rain or shine.

£-££
Vegan

Branches:
Seven Dials Market, Earlham Street, WC2H 9LX 4
Spitalfields, 46-48 Commercial Street, E1 6LT

Gauthier 5

Iconic establishment from the acclaimed chef
21 Romilly Street, W1D 5AF
020 7494 3111
www.gauthiersoho.co.uk
Insta: @gauthierinsoho
Travel: Leicester Square LU
Tue-Sat 17:00-21:30

Alexis Gauthier's achievements and efforts in the world of vegan food are singular - he is perhaps more than anyone else showing that fine dining can be ethical. In this endeavour, he has taken risks in redeveloping his Regency townhouse restaurant in the heart of Soho into a plant-based eating experience unparalleled elsewhere. The formal dining rooms themselves are a lesson in understated luxury, from the fine linen tablecloths to the artistically arranged flowers and Victorian fireplaces. But the food takes centre stage. The delicate cuts of 3D-printed steak and stem cell foie gras made by companies like Redefine Meat, offer a glimpse into the brave new world of synthetic substitutes. There's also a tasting menu of classic French dishes turned vegan, like kombu caviar canapés and seaweed bouillabaisse. Expect to be expertly taken care of, with the provenance of each dish explained in depth, giving you an idea of the dedication to craft that goes into this operation. And despite all this, Gauthier remains reasonably priced given the quality of the food and the dining experience. Their petit dîner of seven courses is priced at £55 per person, whilst the grand dîner of nine is £95 per person, and wine pairings for £45 and £75 per person respectively. This might not just be the best vegan restaurant in London, but the world over.

££££
Vegan

CAVIAR
Freedom!
50g
VEGAN

Govinda's 6

Legendary Hare Krishna canteen

9 Soho Street, W1D 3DL
020 3687 0617
Travel: Tottenham Court LU
Daily 12:00-21:00

Govinda's is a vegetarian restaurant situated on the ground floor of the Radha Krishna Temple between Soho Square and Oxford Street. Their speciality is 'Thali', a style of curry platters where you mix and match smaller portions of different dishes along with rice and bread. They also claim that all their food is karma free - not least because it doesn't contain meat or eggs. Karma is also generated by the dedication to Lord Krishna (known as a 'prasadam') that is offered before being served, meaning blessed with god's mercy.

Here you can expect mixed vegetable curries, chutneys and dahls that are easy on the palate and your wallet (£10 gets you unlimited servings). They also offer non-Indian cuisine like pastas and quiches but their Indian dishes are definitely the better option. Food is served within an unpretentious, canteen-style interior. Govinda's is popular with anyone looking for cheap and cheerful Indian grub whether you follow Hare Krishna or just like the atmosphere of the place. Govinda's is a real London institution and one well worth seeking out - don't forget to admire the model demonstrating the cycle of life at the restaurant's entrance.

£
Vegetarian

Mildred's Soho 7

International cooking at an ethical institution

45 Lexington Street, W1F 9AN
020 7494 1634
www.mildreds.co.uk
Insta: @mildredsrestaurants
Travel: Oxford Circus LU
Mon-Sat 09:00-23:00, Sun 09:00-22:00

Mildred's first opened its doors in 1988 when being vegetarian was considered an eccentric fad. They have always challenged the idea that a meat-free diet was about 'brown mush served in earthenware bowls', instead offering attractive and delicious food from across the world. You can expect to enjoy burritos and their diverse range of burgers alongside South East Asian curries and broths, and many more dishes borrowed from global cuisine. This can all be enjoyed alongside a grown-up selection of drinks, with plenty of organic wines and cocktails to choose from, making Mildred's feel like a far cry from the dull stereotypes of vegetarianism.

Most of their tables are reserved for walk-ins which can involve a wait for a table during peak times. If you're willing to hang about or are fortunate enough to beat the queues, then you can enjoy accessible vegan and vegetarian food inside a casual, modern dining space. This makes for a pleasant evening for devout vegetarians, vegans and curious omnivores alike. Prices reflect the quality of the food and the ambience, with mains fixed at £15 and smaller plates for £5-£8. Mildred's ethos seems to be popular as they have an ever-expanding chain of restaurants across town (see below). One of the longest and most successful plant-focused food establishments in London, Mildred's has a deservedly loyal following.

££
Vegetarian

Branches:
Covent Garden, 79 St Martin's Square, WC2N 4AA
King's Cross, 200 Pentonville Rd, N1 9JP, see p.128
Camden, 9 Jamestown Rd, NW1 7BW
Dalston, 1 Dalston Square, E8 3GU

Neat Burger 8

Start-up king of sustainable eating
33 Old Compton Street, W1D 5JU
www.neat-burger.com
Insta: @neat.burger
Travel: Tottenham Court Road LU
Mon-Thur 11:00-22:00, Fri-Sat 11:00-23:00, Sun 12:00-22:00

It's a familiar story in our tech-happy times – a few friends sit around a table with an idea, and before you know it, they've made a world-beating business. Pretty neat, huh? Well, this too is the premise behind Neat Burger, whose branches are popping up all over town at such a rate you'd be hard-pressed to miss them. Their aim is simple – to make fast-food simultaneously sustainable and desirable, so flexitarians don't feel short-changed when just trying to indulge a little. So, you'll find all the things you'd want to find in your go-to diner – burgers, buffalo nuggets and tater tots. They also have some fresh salad bowls thrown in for good measure and you can wash it down with a Biscoff shake or an Oreo brownie. With prices for burger meals between £5 and £10, this makes them as affordable as many of their high-street equivalents. Neat Burger is mostly a take-out spot but their Miami palm tree aesthetic make it a fun place to eat in.

£
Vegan

Branches:
Camden Lock Market, 44-46 Chalk Farm Road, NW1 8AF
38 Well's Terrace, Finsbury Park, N4 3FP
4 Princes Street, Oxford Circus, W1B 2LE
211 The Balcony, Westfield, Stratford, E20 1GN

POWERED
BY PLANTS

Sagar 9

South Indian staples
31 Catherine Street, WC2B 5JS
020 7836 6377
www.sagarrestaurant.co.uk
Travel: Covent Garden LU
Daily 12:00-21:30

Sagar is a successful South Indian restaurant chain, with branches across Central and West London. They specialise in thalis (mixed curry platter on a steel tray, alongside rice and bread), using tropical fruits that are typical of South Indian cuisine. Mango, lime and especially coconut are the basis of their flavours and dishes are primarily based on lentils. Kootu - a creamy, nutty curry - is always a safe option for the spice averse, but the emphasis here is on good flavour and texture without excessive heat.

Sagar also has a nice selection of traditional sweet things to try, from your standard kulfis to less commonly found fried milk dumplings. The restaurants themselves are all pleasant places to relax and enjoy your meal. Prices are reasonable - expect to spend £20 a head (including drinks) for a comprehensive meal. Offering friendly service and a traditional menu that has remained consistently good over the years, Sagar is a great place for authentic southern Indian cuisine.

££
Vegetarian

Branches:

Hammersmith, 157 King Street, W6 9JT
Harrow, 57 Station Road, HA2 7SR
Fitzrovia, 17a Percy Street, W1T 1DU

Vantra Vegan ⑩

Veteran of vegan cuisine
5 Wardour Street, W1D 6PB
020 7287 5222
www.vantra.co.uk
Insta: @vantralondon
Travel: Leicester Square LU
Tue-Sat 12:00–16:00 & 17:00-22:00,
Sun 12:00–16:00 & 17:00-20:00

Vantra Vegan have been going strong since 1999, thanks to their commitment to making food with health as the central focus. The preparation of dishes is narrowed to three processes: raw foods, which helps retain essential nutrients; fermentation, which adds vital probiotics and other sources of nutrients that can't be found elsewhere; and steaming, which preserves as much of the goodness from the whole food ingredients as possible. The cooking here also completely abstains from refined sugars and gluten, something many more health-conscious consumers are glad to see, with so many unhealthy options dominating the restaurant trade. The menu contains serve-yourself curries, stews and salads full of superfoods, as well as some extras like soy meats, for around £13 per large plate. There's a great smoothie and juice bar offering too, should you only be passing through. If you're after an evening out, keep your eyes peeled for their events, which range from stand-up comedy to debates/Q&A's with vegan influencers.

££
Vegan

★ VEGGIE PRET ★

Veggie Pret ⓫

Pret goes plant-based
35 Broadwick Street, W1F 0DH
020 7932 5274
www.pret.co.uk
Insta: @veggiepret
Travel: Oxford Circus LU
Mon-Fri 07:00-19:00, Sat 09:00-16:00

Amid the boom of plant-based eating in recent years, Pret A Manger emerged as a game changer, being one of the first corporate giants to make a real commitment to vegetarian and vegan food. Veggie Pret has been so successful that it now has four branches and has plans for further expansion. You'll find a generous array of veggie and vegan ready-to-eat foods like sandwiches, salads and finger bites, as well as all Pret's classic hot and cold beverages (made plant-based). Some firm favourites include their meatless meatball wrap and the chef's Italian Salad. They also have a vegan baked section where they offer berry croissants and rocky roads. The company uses mostly natural ingredients, donates unsold food to charities combating food poverty and is making a concerted effort to eliminate plastic packaging. Veggie Pret offers among the cheapest veggie and vegan food in London, with nearly everything costing less than £5 and plenty for less than £3. Veggie Pret marks an important and welcome shift in our eating habits.

£
Vegetarian

Branches:
21 Exmouth Market, EC1R 4QD
62 Fenchurch Street, EC3M 4BE
57 Great Eastern Street, EC2A 3QD

MARYLEBONE & MAYFAIR

1. 123V
2. Crosstown Doughnuts, Picton Place
3. The Gate Marylebone
4. Neat Burger, Oxford Circus
5. Plants
6. Tendril
7. Wulf & Lamb

Shops:

A) Stella McCartney, see p.329

REGENT'S PARK
BAKER STREET
PARK CRES
MARYLEBONE RD
PORTLAND PL
DEVONSHIRE ST
MARYLEBONE HIGH ST
YORK ST
PADDINGTON ST
WEYMOUTH ST
BAKER ST
GLOUCESTER PL
NEW CAVENDISH ST
BLANDFORD ST
LANGHAM PL
Wallace Collection
GEORGE ST
MARYLEBONE LN
CAVENDISH SQ
PORTMAN SQUARE
WIGMORE ST
JAMES ST
HENRIETTA PL
OXFORD CIRCUS
SEYMOUR ST
OXFORD ST
BOND STREET
HANOVER ST
MARBLE ARCH
DUKE ST
NEW BOND ST
BROOK ST
REGENT ST
CONDUIT ST
SAVILLE ROW
GROSVENOR SQUARE
DAVIES ST
PARK ST
OLD BOND ST
VIGO ST
PICCADILLY CIRCUS
Royal Academy
BERKELEY SQUARE
PARK LANE
SOUTH AUDLEY ST
FARM ST
HILL ST
PICCADILLY
JERMYN ST
HYDE PARK
GREEN PARK
CURZON ST
SHEPHERD ST
HYDE PARK CORNER

3
W

123V ❶

Sustainable sushi from Michelin-starred chef Alexis Gauthier

Terrace & Lower Ground Floor at Fenwick,
63 New Bond St, W1S 1RQ
020 8132 9088
www.123vegan.co.uk
Insta: @123vegan_w1
Travel: Bond Street LU
Mon-Wed 12:00-18:00, Thur-Sat 12:00-20:00, Sun 12:00-15:30

Think of this as a sister site to the eponymous Gauthier, the Michelin-starred establishment that sent shockwaves through the restaurant world when it became fully vegan back in 2021 (see p.44). Except this is a sister that loves sushi, so much so that you can not only make your own in a fancy Japanese machine, but also enjoy a bottomless supply every day except Sunday from 4pm, for £30 per person. It's all vegan with flavours including tuna, salmon-avocado, California rolls and prawn – all made from things like banana blossom or tofu.

If sushi isn't your thing, then the cafeteria comes stocked aplenty with salads, bowls of pesto pasta or yakisoba, burgers, bao buns and breakfasts like the 'Full Vinglish' or pancakes – you really can't accuse them of not having something for everyone here. Mains range between £12 and £17, reflecting the prices of this upmarket location. The eatery itself is remarkably swanky with the added appeal of its outdoor terrace. If your meal here leaves you feeling inspired, you can take one of their vegan sushi-making courses too, so you can make it at home as easy as 123V.

££-£££
Vegan

Crosstown Doughnuts ❷

Doughnuts to die for
5-6 Picton Place, W1U 1BL
www.crosstowndoughnuts.com
Insta: @crosstown
Travel: Bond Street LU
Daily 10:00-20:00

When the Crosstown team started selling their hybrid sourdough doughnuts on Leather Lane market in 2014, it seems they knew they were destined for 'crosstown' greatness. Indeed, these days you're unlikely to be more than a stone's throw from these goodies. The Marylebone branch is the only one that is 100% vegan, offering all the devilish doughnuts imaginable, completely guilt-free. But all branches have a range of vegan options. A glance at their Instagram is likely to seal the deal, as these doughnuts aren't limited to the dull sugar-dusted varieties. Instead, think multi-coloured glazes, oozing jams and crumbled toppings aplenty. Using a mixture of plant-based alternatives like chia seeds, coconut butter and tofu, they've achieved vegan doughnuts that really rival their dairy doppelgängers. You can enjoy a range of drinks alongside them, including kombucha, chocolate milks and coffee from the Caravan Roastery. Doughnuts cost between £3 and £5 but beware, you'll definitely be coming back for more.

£
Vegan

Branches:
Soho, 4 Broadwick Street, W1F 0DA
Fitzrovia, 13 Newman Street, W1T 1PB
Shoreditch, 157 Brick Lane, E1 6SB
And many more, see their website for the full list.

SSTOWN
CROS

The Gate Marylebone ❸

An entry point for ethical eating

22-24 Seymour Place, Marylebone, W1H 7NL
020 7724 6656
www.thegaterestaurants.com
Tue & Wed 17:00-23:00, Thur-Fri 12:00-15:00 & 17:00-23:00, Sat 10:00-23:00, Sun 10:00-21:30

The Gate company is now rightly recognised as an institution for fine vegetarian food. The founders' Indian and Iraqi heritage shines through many of the dishes, although the menu extends to anything from aubergine schnitzel to artichoke gnocchi. Main meals are priced between £15 and £20, while starters and sides settle for around half as much. The dining space is a refreshingly grown-up environment making it perfect for a special occasion. We recommend you take time over the extensive drinks menu that has everything from mocktails to vegan wines.

£££
Vegetarian

Branches:
51 Queen Caroline Street, W6 9QL (see p.154)
370 St John St, EC1V 4NN (see p.120)

Branch

Neat Burger ❹

Start-up king of sustainable eating

4 Princes Street, Oxford Circus, W1B 2LE
www.neat-burger.com
see review on p.50

Plants 5

Gluten-free goodness by Deliciously Ella
18 Weighhouse Street, W1K 5AH
020 7436 9436
www.deliciouslyella.com/plants
Insta: @deliciouslyella
Travel: Bond Street LU
Mon-Fri 08:00-11:15 & 12:00-20:45,
Sat 09:00-11:15 & 12:00-20:45, Sun 09:00-11:15 & 12:00-16:30

Deliciously Ella was opened by Ella Mills, the cookery author and entrepreneur, in a joint venture with her husband and business partner. They've successfully brought the plant-based philosophy of Deliciously Ella to life in this physical store. Open all day, it serves breakfasts and lunches, with the former tending to lean on the sweet stuff, like fruity porridges, pancakes and puddings, and the latter featuring dishes from around the world. You can expect to enjoy an array of salads, risottos and ragùs, as well as a variety of chillies and curries. These are reasonably priced, especially considering the average price point in the area and of other health food alternatives. Breakfasts cost between £6 and £13, and most mains around £18. Fittingly, the interior is an Instagrammer's delight - Scandinavian minimalist décor, plenty of natural light and rustic wooden tables will help you get that perfect picture.

£-££
Vegan
Gluten-free

Tendril Kitchen 6

Affordable tasting menus
5 Princes Street, W1B 2LQ
0784 2797 541
www.tendrilkitchen.co.uk
Insta: @tendril_kitchen
Travel: Oxford Street LU
Mon 17:00-22;00, Tue-Fri 12:30-15:30 & 17:00-22:00,
Sat 12:30-22:00, Sun 12:30-17:00

Few vegan restaurants have managed to cater to the demand for fine dining that is the norm for this corner of Mayfair. That is, until now. Tendril is forking up the sort of food you'd expect from the swankier restaurants across Soho, but for a fraction of the cost. Tasting menus take you on a tour of blue corn tostadas, crispy celeriac terrine, arancini and Massaman curry, for either £24pp at lunch or £39pp at dinner (you can also order à la carte). They self-style as 'accidentally' vegan, which does mean that not every dish on the menu is plant-based (you can choose between vegan and vegetarian menus), but also explains why the place is so approachable. The food is remarkable whichever option you choose and the space feels like a restaurant should, with marble-top tables and attractive lighting, appealing crockery and smart service. This is definitely a venue for a special occasion.

£££
Vegetarian

Branch

Wulf & Lamb 7

No predator, no prey
66 Chiltern Street, W1U 4EJ
www.wulfandlamb.com
see review on p.165

CLASSIC V
£7.00
CLASSIC V
FACON CHEESEBURGER
our classic burger with strips of crispy maple facon, a slice of mature cheddar vegan cheese, served on a warm bun with salad leaves, slow roasted tomato relish, pickles, onion and creamy burger sauce.
£7.50
VEGAN

THE HOLY SMOKE
our classic burger with a slice of smoked vegan cheese, served on a warm bun with BBQ sauce, smokey chipotle mayo & grilled onions
£7.50
Ingredients: British barley, tomato concentrate, parsley, soy sauce, miso, herbs, mushrooms, wheat, vegan mayo, mustard, gluten

NORTH

CAMDEN, CHALK FARM, KENTISH TOWN & PRIMROSE HILL

1. Clean Kitchen Camden
2. The Fields Beneath
3. Hawraman: My Village Café Bar
4. Helma
5. Magic Falafel
6. Manna
7. Mildred's Camden
8. Neat Burger
9. Powerplant
10. Purezza
11. Rudy's Vegan Diner
12. Temple of Camden
13. VBurger
14. What the Pitta!
15. Vegan Planet

Shops:

A) Earth Natural Foods, see p.334

KENTISH TOWN
BELSIZE PARK
HAVERSTOCK HILL
MAITLAND PARK VILLAS
QUEEN'S CRES
BASSET ST
MALDEN RD
GRAFTON RD
HOLMES RD
ISLIP ST
CAVERSHAM RD
GAISFORD ST
PATSHULL RD
KENTISH TOWN RD
KENTISH TOWN WEST
PRINCE OF WALES RD
ROCHESTER RD
CASTLE HAVEN RD
HARMOOD ST
ETON RD
CHALK FARM
CHALK FARM RD
ADELAIDE RD
HARTLAND RD
HAWLEY RD
CAMDEN ROAD
KING HENRY'S RD
Camden Market
AINGER RD
PRIMROSE HILL RD
GLOUCESTER AVE
FITZROY RD
REGENT'S PARK RD
Regent's Canal
JAMESTOWN RD
CAMDEN TOWN
ROYAL COLLEGE ST
CAMDEN RD
OVAL RD
INVERNESS ST
BAYHAM ST
PRATT ST
PARKWAY
ARLINGTON RD
CAMDEN HIGH RD
ALBERT RD
DELANCEY ST
PARK VILLAGE EAST
MORNINGTON CRESCENT
REGENT'S PARK
OUTER CIRCLE
ALBANY ST
A
1
2
3
4
5
6
7
8
9
10
11
12
13
14
15

The Clean Kitchen Camden ❶

Junk food but cleaned up

198 Camden High Street, NW1 8QP
020 3089 8330
www.cleankitchen.club
Insta: @cleankitchenuk
Travel: Camden Town LU
Mon-Wed 11:00-18:00, Thur-Sun 10:00-20:00

To anyone who's been around to see London's vegan restaurant scene emerge over the last few years, Clean Kitchen will be very familiar. Their menu takes a tour of the staples of a plant-based menu - smoothies, acai and salad bowls, burgers - basically as much faux meat as you can eat between two pieces of bread. This is fast food after all! They've stated explicitly they aim to become the 'plant-based McDonald's' - so expect all manner of fries, nuggets and desserts like cheesecake too. But as their name suggests, cleanliness runs through this all, from the sustainability of their ingredients, and into the space as well - it's a large shipping container transformed into a glass box. In truth, it might be a while until they dethrone the cheapest of fast-food chains, with all their burgers costing close to £10 and sides around half of that. But then again, you don't get luxuries like truffle mayo or smoked 'salmon' there, so stop by and give them a try to see for yourself.

£-££
Vegan

Branches:
126 New Kings Road, SW6 4L
172 Portobello Road, W11 2EB
Boxpark Wembley, Wembley Park, HA9 0JT
126 New Kings Road, London, SW6 4LZ

The Fields Beneath ❷

Friendly community café
52a Prince of Wales Road, NW5 3LN
020 7424 8838
www.thefieldsbeneath.com
Insta: @fieldsbeneath
Travel: Kentish Town West LO, Chalk Farm LU
Mon-Fri 07:30-16:00, Sat 08:00-17:00, Sun 09:00-17:00

You can't ask for much more from a vegan café than The Fields Beneath. It's a warm, laid-back space offering delicious wraps, burgers, sandwiches and sausage rolls, as well as sweet pastries and a bevvy of beverages and it's all completely cruelty-free. Since deciding to ditch dairy, their food has really come into its own, and now offers some of the best café staples to be found in London.

With their ever-changing seasonal menu, they've earned a devoted crowd of regulars. Tuck into one of their delicious sandwiches, be it their ALT (aubergine, lettuce, tomato) bagel or their chimichurri squash sandwich, and enjoy the vibe of this sweet little community. You don't have to break the bank here with their signature rarebit croissant for £5.50 and plain ones for £2.80, lunch for £8.80 and plenty of hot drinks and cakes for just £3 to £5. Trying their single-origin Colombian coffee is a must. They also host a natural wine-tasting session every full moon for £25 per person.

The café is located under the railway arches of Kentish Town West Station, one of a number of small but eclectic businesses that include the Camden Town Brewery (all their beers are vegan too!) and Lunar Cycles. You'll be hard pressed to miss it though, as they've left an array of comical road signs to draw in the uninitiated. One of London's best vegan eateries.

£
Vegan

Hawraman: My Village Café Bar ❸

Cosy Kurdish café

38 Chalk Farm Road, NW1 8AJ
020 7813 2908
www.hawramancamdencafe.com
Travel: Kentish Town West Overground
Tue-Thur & Sun 11:00-21.30, Fri-Sat 11:00-22.30

This Camden café is a rustic eatery serving a selection of staple Kurdish dishes in a casual, yet cosy interior. You can expect to find things like baba ganoush, falafel and halloumi salads, alongside a range of lighter dishes and drinks. We recommend their 'My Grandma's Soup' served with toasted wholemeal bread for only £6 – they even let you try a sample to test the flavours (they won't disappoint). Everything is vegetarian, but they also serve some vegan and gluten-free options.

The tables are spread out in a communal style, and the owners encourage sharing space with your neighbours, so don't count on an intimate escape here. What you can expect is that the food will be fresh, good quality and won't leave you feeling guilty or bloated afterwards. They also have outdoor seating at the back and front for when the weather is fine, plus a spot by the fireplace for when it's not. The prices are reasonable for Camden with mains costing between £6 and £15. It's a pleasant place to eat and serves food that feels a lot more authentic than the usual fare in the area, which is largely dominated now by big chains.

£-££
Vegetarian

Helma Café

Multicultural community café
57A Jamestown Road, Camden, NW1 7DP
www.helmalondon.com
Insta: @helmalondon
Travel: Camden Town LU
Mon-Fri 08:00-18:00, Sat-Sun 09:00-17:00

This cosy little café is nestled within Camden's Triyoga Studio and is remarkably popular with those who practice there and are looking for some post-exercise nourishment. There are quite a few lycra-clad customers but this place also offers a warm welcome to less flexible members of the general public, who just want to sample the delicious veggie food on offer. Helma used to be called the Nectar Café, but the change in name and ownership has been nothing but an improvement. Tess and Kosta have applied their years of experience in the vegetarian restaurant trade to make this a great place to visit for simple, well-prepared food such as granola with Kent honey and stewed apples or a hearty bowl of dahl that is freshly made on site and comes with Ararat flatbread. This little café space is a worthy addition to Camden's veggie scene but it offers just a flavour of the Helma experience. For a more extensive menu, complete with a selection of natural wines, you'll need to head east to their much larger Hackney establishment where Tess's love of fermented veg and her native Swedish culinary tradition is given wider expression (see p.262). Still, if you're in Camden and looking for some yogic calm and delicious veggie food, this is a strong recommendation.

££
Vegetarian

MAGIC
FALAFEL

Magic Falafel ❺

Fast food falafel

Unit 312-313, Camden Lock Market, NW1 8AH
0748 264 6499
www.magicfalafel.co.uk
Insta: @magic_falafel
Travel: Camden Town LU
Daily 10:30-19:30

For years falafel has been the go-to vegetarian fast food, long before seitan chicken wings and tofish captured our imaginations. Many an establishment has claimed that theirs is the gold standard, but with a plethora of Middle Eastern and speciality eateries now all over London, it takes a lot to stand out from the crowd. And doing just that is Magic Falafel - a relative newcomer with a rapidly growing reputation for serving top-quality fritters and pittas. They also do salad boxes jam-packed with tasty fresh vegetables, with the fried aubergines worthy of special mention. With a couple of locations in Camden's Lock and Stables Markets, they're hard to miss amid the foodie furore, especially as they're a vegan and gluten-free establishment. They're not cheap, with pittas and salad boxes between £9.50 and £10.50, but these guys would give most local kebab shops a run for their money.

Aside from the all-important tahini and houmous, they also serve a good curry sauce or chilli to accompany your meal. If you're in town and up for a spot of alfresco dining, don't forget to bear Magic Falafel in mind, or if London's weather keeps you indoors then Deliveroo is at hand to help.

£
Vegan
Gluten-free

Manna 6

International fine dining
4 Erskine Road, NW3 3AJ
0778 8835 892
www.mannalondon.co.uk
Insta: @mannalondon
Travel: Chalk Farm LU
Weds-Thur 06:30-22:00, Fri 06:30-10:30,
Sat 12:30-22:30, Sun 12:30-16:30

A stone's throw from Primrose Hill is the oldest surviving vegetarian restaurant in London, which celebrated its 50th anniversary in 2017. Manna is now 100% vegan and looks entirely different from its origins in north London's 1960's counterculture. Today it offers a more refined dining experience than most other plant-based eateries in the capital. A curated selection of dishes from world cuisine is on the menu, with Jamaican stews featuring alongside mezzes – and the chef's daily special is nearly always one to look out for. Lots of raw and gluten-free options are available too, in keeping with Manna's desire to promote healthy eating.

The space isn't bedecked with chandeliers, but the white tablecloth service during the evenings makes for a more upmarket vegan dinner date than is otherwise readily available. Mains are fairly expensive in comparison to other London vegan eateries, at £15 a head, and for a full course meal, you should expect to spend at least £30 per head. Manna's origins can be seen in the photos scattered about the restaurant showing the restaurant's early days. The place may have changed but there is a continuity here that we hope endures for many years to come.

£££
Vegan

Branch

Mildred's Camden 7

International

9 Jamestown Road, Camden Town, NW1 7BW

www.mildreds.co.uk/camden

See review on p.48

Neat Burger 8

Start-up king of sustainable eating

Camden Lock Market, 44b-46 Chalk Farm Road, NW1 8AF
020 4580 1227
www.neat-burger.com
Insta: @neat.burger
Travel: Camden Town LU
Sun-Thur 11:00-21:00, Fri-Sat 11:00-22:00

This is the Camden outlet of Neat Burger, who have rapidly expanded in recent years and now have branches across London. The formula is simple: to make fast-food simultaneously sustainable and desirable, so flexitarians don't feel short-changed when just trying to indulge a little. This offers the same reliable menu of burgers, buffalo nuggets, tater tots, as well as some salad bowls thrown in for good measure and you can wash it down with a Biscoff shake or an Oreo brownie. With prices for items between £5 and £10, they are as affordable as many of their high-street equivalents, but their Miami palm tree aesthetic makes them a considerably more enjoyable establishment to eat in.

£
Vegan

Branches:
38 Well's Terrace, Finsbury Park, N4 3FP
4 Princes Street, Oxford Circus, W1B 2LE
211 The Balcony, Westfield, Stratford, E20 1GN
33 Old Compton Street, W1D 5JU

Power Plant 9

A meatless medley

89 Chalk Farm Road, NW1 8AR
0737 680 9248
www.powerplant.global
Travel: Chalk Farm LU
Mon-Thur 07:00-23:00, Fri & Sat 07:00-23:30, Sun 07:00-22:30

This latest addition to Camden's vegan arsenal is the restaurant of a hotel in the area, which has kept this spot somewhat of a hidden gem. And inside it's a veritable treasure trove, with just about every desire catered for on the menu. Whilst their breakfast offering covers the expected classics like granola, tofu scramble and BLTs, costing between £6 and £10, their lunch and dinner service navigates dishes as diverse as dumplings, pakora, arancini, burgers, risotto and burritos. Small plates and sides will set you back between £5 and £7 whilst larger ones go for £11-£12. If you have room, the desserts include salted caramel brownies and coconut pudding and are around a fiver. This, along with the attractive presentation in earthenware dishes and plant-filled interior, makes this a great place for a date or just for casual dining when hanging out in Camden.

££
Vegan

NEW AMSTERDAM

Purezza ⑩

The country's original vegan pizzeria
45-47 Parkway, NW1 7PN
020 3884 0078
www.purezza.co.uk
Insta: @purezzauk
Travel: Camden Town LU
Mon-Thur 12:00-22:00, Fri-Sat 12:00-22:30, Sun 12:00-21:00

Not all good things come from London, and Purezza is here to prove it. Born in Brighton, they're the UK's first vegan pizzeria, and have enjoyed such success that they've now got four branches - in Manchester, Bristol and here in Camden. With over 10 styles of pizza on the menu, as well as pasta dishes, sides and desserts, Purezza offers a complete vegan take on the Italian dining experience. Expect your favourite indulgences like lasagne and tiramisu, classics like margherita and pepperoni, as well as their signature pizzas like Parmigiana Party (Aubergine Parmigiana on a pizza - need I say more?).

They now offer small plates so you can try a selection of mini pizzas, sides like slow-baked meatballs or their famous doughballs, and pasta. The deal of three dishes for £18 means you needn't choose between pizza or pasta. But bear in mind that the evening menu has more pizza options if that is your purezza desire. Mains are £10 to £15, and sides and sweet things are reasonably priced. There's plenty of space in the simply furnished restaurant, with views of the wood burning oven and the chefs working away in the busy kitchen. Purezza are a great example of the transformation in London's vegan scene and judging from their busy Camden outpost, they are here to stay.

££
Vegan

Rudy's Vegan Diner ⓫

Meat-free American diner
729-731 Camden Lock, Chalk Farm, NW1 8AH
020 3383 0222
www.rudysvegan.com
Insta: @rudysDVD
Travel: Camden Town LU
Mon-Thur 12:00-21:00, Fri 12:00-21:30, Sat-Sun 11:00-21:30

Doing veganism the dirty way has become popular among many followers of the lifestyle, not least on account of the tired association with salads and bean stews. As you might be able to tell from their name, Rudy's is one such establishment, and they're doing their bit for those ditching meat, while unabashedly shouting it from the rafters.

A glance at their food shows they're doing it the right way. No longer do you have to forgo stacked-up Reuben sandwiches, buffalo wings or 'dirty dogz', for all manner of meaty and messy things can be found here. The open kitchen allows you to see your food being prepared and there is plenty of seating inside and also outside - looking out onto Stables Market - for when the weather is good. It's a tad more expensive than competing junk food eateries, with burgers costing around £8, sides for around half of this and meal deals for £10. We're not complaining that Camden Market has another vegan eatery though, and the loyal crowd around here aren't either.

£-££
Vegan

Fryin' Daily
TEMPLE
LDN OF VGN
SEITAN
Camden & Hackney
EAT IN OR TAKE AWAY

Temple of Seitan ⓬

Vegan fried chicken
43 Parkway, NW1 7PN
www.templeofseitan.co.uk
Insta: @templeofseitan
Travel: Camden Town LU
Daily 12:00-22:00

Sister store to the Seitan outpost in Hackney that is London's first vegan chicken shop, the Temple of Camden brings a slightly more dine-in vibe to the brand, with a coolly designed space and extra indoor seating. They also have more options, including 'hamburgers', pastries and hot drinks. This is one of the best ways to indulge in something that feels naughty, but isn't, and makes for some fairly Instagrammable grub too. Seitan - essentially a wheat cake - by and large, has the taste, texture and appearance of chicken, and when wedged between a bun and with all the extras you really can't tell the difference. This is a little less the case with the wings, but these are still a tasty treat alongside a box of chips and a soft drink. At between £5 and £7 for burgers, wings and wraps (and considerably less for sides and sweet things), the Temple is price-competitive with KFC, and is so much better on all fronts, showing that you don't need chicken to satisfy those Kentucky fried cravings. One of our favourite vegan food brands, Temple of Seitan's three outposts are perfect places to eat, whatever the weather.

£
Vegan

Branches:
Temple of Hackney, 5 Morning Lane, E9 6NA (see p. 284)
419 Coldharbour Lane, SW9 8LH (see p.204)

VBurger ⓭

Vegan burgers in Camden Market

Unit 305, Camden Lock Market,
215-216 Chalk Farm Road, NW1 8AF
07412 629 102
www.vburger.co.uk
Insta: @vburgercamden_
Travel: Camden Town LU & LO
Mon-Thur 11:00-20:00, Fri-Sat 11:00-21:00

Among a handful of meat-free eateries popping up in and around the Camden Lock, VBurger has made a lasting impression with their signature charcoal sesame buns. Unlike other vegan burger spots, they have a decidedly diverse menu, with a variety of patties to choose from – so whether you're a seitan fanatic or prefer wholefoods, there is something for everyone (they even offer gluten-free buns). The falafel or 'seitan schnitzel' burger with a Coke and onion rings will set you back £14, but if you want an 'up beet' burger or moving mountains hotdog individually, they cost £8.95-9.95. If you'd like a delicious syrupy milkshake to wash it all down with, they offer chocolate Oreo and banana Biscoff flavours alongside classics like vanilla, all for a reasonable £6. There is a small countertop facing the kitchen where you can sit down and eat, but don't expect an intimate occasion or sheltered seating when visiting. VBurger is an appetising vegan alternative to the local fast-food joints in the area and one very much in keeping with Camden's frenetic atmosphere.

£
Vegan

What the Pitta!
WHATTHEPITTA.COM
What the Pitta!
WHATTHEPITTA.COM

What the Pitta! 14

London's first vegan kebab shop
89-91 Bayham Street, NW1 0AG
0798 3095 801
www.whatthepitta.com
Insta: @whatthepitta
Travel: Camden Town LU
Sun-Thur 12:00-21:00, Fri-Sat 12:00-22:00

A fitting name for a restaurant serving kebabs that'll make you exclaim just how meaty their döner dopplegängers taste while managing to be 100% vegan. What the Pitta's success has seen them extend their roots beyond Brick Lane and they've now set up their third venture in town - a nu-age kebab shop in Camden. The menu is small but has everything you really need - döner boxes, lahmacuns, tzatziki and mezze, as well as soft drinks, beers, and baklava for the sweet-toothed. The chunks of spicy soya in What the Pitta's boxes are full of flavour, and with pitta, salad and chips are just as good, as the meaty alternative. Carnivores have no excuse and anyone who thought this stuff was reserved for nights out with inhibited decision-making can think again. Prices are competitive, with a main, side and drink costing £12 and to make that drink a beer (in the true spirit of the kebab shop) then it's only an extra quid. The spaces themselves are much alike, with enough seating for those wanting to eat in and minimal décor. What the Pitta! is the perfect antidote to the capital's meaty street food.

£
Vegan

Branches:
Box Park Croydon, Unit 9, 99 George Street, CR0 1LD
53 Brick Lane, Shoreditch, E1 6PU

Vegan Planet ⑮

Vegan Cantonese that's out of this world

11 Parkway, NW1 7PG
020 7482 0656
www.veganplanetuk.com
Insta: @veganplanetcamden
Travel: Camden Town LU
Daily 11:00-23:00

Few adopted dishes have been as universally adored as Chinese duck pancakes. I imagine many a vegan has missed this classic when out dining. Well, they should miss it no longer, as its back on the menu for all plant-based patrons at Vegan Planet, the capital's first restaurant to make Cantonese cuisine, including dim sum, available to those entirely eschewing meat (Vegan planet is actually the second life of a former vegan restaurant pioneer - Dou Dou). Expect all those familiar favourites like kung pao 'chicken' or 'beef' in black bean sauce, wonton soup and steamed dumplings, sesame toast and soy-sautéed pak choi. This is all made possible through two key ingredients, which are both essential to Chinese cuisine - tofu and seitan. The former was, depending on who you ask, either invented during the Han dynasty as a potential elixir of immortality or taken from Mongolian tribes' cheese-making. The latter dates back 1500 years to Buddhist culinary practices. Prices for mains hover around £10, which makes this competitive with their meaty rivals. They serve vegan wines, beers and spirits too, so Vegan Planet should definitely be in your orbit when organising an evening out in Camden.

££
Vegan

HAMPSTEAD

Rani

Gujarati neighbourhood restaurant
7 Long Lane, Church End, N3 2PR
020 8349 2636
www.rani.uk.com
Insta: @raniveguk
Travel: Finchley Central LU
Daily 11:00-15:00 & 18:00-22:00

Rani is a popular and long-standing local Indian restaurant that has been serving the curry needs of Finchleyites for over 30 years. Specialising in vegetarian Gujarati cuisine, they've got plenty of dishes to try out, from your typical chickpea and aubergine fare to less commonly found spiced bananas in gravy. Of course, this can all be enjoyed alongside naans, daals and rice dishes in a pleasantly decorated interior that makes for a nice spot to relax and sample authentic Gujarati food. If you simply can't choose between their mouth-watering curries, you needn't, as they also offer a plentiful buffet during the dinner service and all day on the weekends for between £11.95 and £22.95 per head. But those with a hearty appetite will find their 'all you can eat' policy great value. Perhaps not one to travel far for, but a sound option when in the area, Rani certainly knows how to make a good curry.

££
Vegetarian

HOLLOWAY, CROUCH HILL & TUFNELL PARK

1. Cookies and Scream
2. Engocha
3. EZ & Moss
4. Healthy Wealthy
5. Jai Krishna
6. Keren View
7. Loving Hut

Shops:

A) The Third Estate, see p.336

Elthorne Park
CROUCH HILL
STROUD GREEN ST
ST JOHN'S WAY
ARCHWAY RD
HIGHGATE HILL
HANLEY RD
ASHBROOK RD
DARTMOUTH PARK HILL
ARCHWAY
HORNSEY RD
TOLLINGTON PARK
FONTHILL RD
FINSBURY PARK
UPPER HOLLOWAY
SUSSEX WAY
ST THOMAS'S RD
HOLLOWAY RD
Whittington Park
Dartmouth Park
JUNCTION RD
WINDSOR RD
SEVEN SISTERS RD
TOLLINGTON RD
STATION RD
TYTHERTON RD
Gillespie Park
TUFNELL PARK
TUFNELL PARK RD
ARSENAL
HUDDLESTON RD
HOLLOWAY RD
HORNSEY RD
DRAYTON PARK
HIGHBURY HILL
FORTESS RD
ANSON RD
PANKHURST RD
CAMDEN RD
CALEDONIAN RD
BRECKNOCK RD
DALMENY AV
HILLMARTON RD
DRAYTON PARK
KENTISH TOWN
HOLLOWAY ROAD
LEIGHTON RD
TORRIANO AVE
CAMDEN RD
HUNGERFORD RD
GEORGE'S RD
RONALDS RD
HOLLOWAY RD
ISLIP ST
BARTHOLOMEW RD
CALEDONIAN ROAD
NORTH RD
MACKENZIE RD
Paradise Park
Highbury Fields
KENTISH TOWN RD
PATSHULL RD
CAMDEN ROAD
CAMDEN PARK
Caledonian Park
WESTBOURNE RD
LIVERPOOL RD
ROMAN WAY
MARKET RD
CALEDONIAN RD
HIGHBURY & ISLINGTON
CAMDEN RD
YORK WAY
BREWERY RD
BLUNDELL ST
OFFORD RD
CAMDEN ROAD
AGAR GROVE
CALEDONIAN ROAD & BARNSBY
BEWDLEY ST

Cookies and Scream ❶

Guilt-free gluttony

130 Holloway Road, N7 8JE
www.cookiesandscream.com
Insta: @cookiesandscreambakery
Travel: Holloway Road LU
Wed-Fri 12:30-18:30, Sat-Sun 12:00-19:00

Founded in Camden, Cookies and Scream has thrived since their move to Holloway Road. A vegan, gluten-free bakery and desserts diner, they offer a bewildering choice of flavours of dairy-free cakes, cookies and shakes. Health food is strictly off the agenda – their delicious produce is sugar-rich, and unsuitable for anyone with nut or soya intolerances.

For a small outlet, Cookies and Scream have developed quite a following, which has surely been helped by their Instagram page showing off doughnuts slathered in thick chocolate sauce, and Victoria sponges oozing with jam. Their popularity translates into how fast the day's batches sell out, so get down early if you can. The interior is limited to a few small tables and chairs to perch on, but there is outdoor seating on sunny days. The prices are very reasonable – expect to pay £2 to £3 for hot beverages, £4 for milkshakes and between £3 and £5 for a generous dessert. If you're looking to pig out then Cookies and Scream is really worth a visit for any vegan, veggie or omnivore with a sweet tooth.

£
Vegan
Gluten-free

Engocha ❷

Authentic Ethiopian cuisine
143 Fortess Road, NW5 2HR
020 7485 3838
Insta: @engochacafe
Travel: Tufnell Park LU
Daily 12:00-18:00

Engocha is an Ethiopian diner that doles out quality grub, that also happens to be healthy, vegan, and inexpensive. They serve traditional stews alongside rice or injera - a doughy flatbread native to the Horn of Africa - that can be enjoyed as a platter of five dishes to be shared between two for £25 or individually for £14. Or if there's a curry you already know and love, individual dishes are priced between £11 and £14. These curried stews bring together an abundance of leafy greens and legumes, with an intriguing mix of herbs and spices. Everything is gluten-free, nut-free and vegan. A meal in this calming environment is guaranteed to leave you feeling satisfied and healthy.

Engocha takes great pride in its Ethiopian coffee which is hand roasted to order and is deliciously strong. It arrives the way it is traditionally served, with smoking frankincense. The dining space is a simple one, with just a few tables and chairs, and no toilet, but the atmosphere is friendly and relaxed and the food more than compensates for the spartan decor.

£
Vegan
Gluten-free

EZ & Moss ③

Easy-going neighbourhood café

183 Holloway Road, N7 8LX
www.ezmoss.co.uk
Insta: @ezandMoss
Travel: Holloway Road LU
Tue-Fri 08:00-16:00, Sat 09:00-16:00

When looking to escape the bustle of N7's Holloway Road, EZ & Moss is a welcome world away from neighbouring seedy bookies and kebab shops. A tranquil indie café attracting a different crowd of locals to those filling the terraces on match day. Here you'll find a range of great hot beverages and freshly made vegan and vegetarian foods. Sweet treats sit in harmony with healthier meals – enjoy a fluffy muffin and matcha latte, or follow a light salad or veggie breakfast with an AllPress coffee.

The menu changes often and features a daily rotation of specials, but salads, stews, burgers and brunch dishes are regulars, all full of flavour and colour. We're keenest on their fruity porridges and granolas. EZ & Moss is an inviting setting, with a minimal, white-walled interior, wooden surfaces and charming details like light bulb saltshakers. The service is friendly and personal too and you can see your food being prepared behind the counter as you wind down with a coffee. The pricing is fair and the atmosphere relaxed and friendly, making this one of our favourite north London cafés.

£
Vegetarian

HEALTHY
WEALTHY
VEGAN

Healthy Wealthy 4

Top-tier Indian thalis and sweets
10 Brecknock Road, N7 0DD
020 7700 0777
www.healthywealthyvegan.co.uk
Insta: @healthywealthy
Travel: Caledonian Road LU
Mon-Sat 11.30-21:00

This little north London establishment is one of the best spots for getting thali in the city, and it's all vegan and almost entirely gluten-free. To the uninitiated, thalis are steel tray platters of curry that are great for getting a taste of everything and are traditionally eaten with the hands, using rice and bread to mop up the vegetable and legume-rich curries. The dishes at Healthy Wealthy are some of the most wholesome and tasty around, and if you look beyond the no-frills set up, you'll have found yourself a little gem. Expect saag and daal, bhel puri, samosas and pakoras aplenty, all of which can be enjoyed inexpensively. You can tuck into a thali for as little as £9 with extras for around £1. There is also a selection of Indian sweets and cakes available for around £2 each. This is a solid local option when seeking out good Indian fare and is just opposite Third Estate for all your vegan, ethical clothing and footwear needs (see p. 336).

£
Vegan

Jai Krishna 5

Crouch Hill's favourite curry house

161 Stroud Green Rd, N4 3PZ

020 7272 1680

Travel: Crouch Hill LO

Mon-Sat 12:00-14:00 & 17:30-22:30

Stroud Green residents are lucky to have such a popular local Indian restaurant on their doorstep, and one which is also among the cheapest - curries start from as little as £4.50. The menu is diverse and takes inspiration from across the Indian subcontinent. Some of our favourites are heavier dahls from the North, and mango and buttermilk curries, called kalan, from the South. These are of course best enjoyed alongside a range of side dishes and snacks that are as inexpensive as the mains. For a comprehensive meal expect to pay around £8.

The space is intriguing - colourful renditions of Krishna and Christ stand side by side against red walls, giving a taste of India's colourful diversity. There's no meat on the menu but vegans should double-check if ghee and paneer feature in their preferred dish. The only downside we can find about this cheap and cheerful eatery is that it's a bit out of the way, but you'll still need to book at weekends. Despite the trek, it's worth making your way to N4 with your own bottle of booze to see what Jai Krishna's is all about.

£

Vegetarian

Keren View 6

Ethical Eritrean eating

201 Holloway Road, N7 8DJ
0795 825 2822
Travel: Holloway Road LU
Daily 12:00-22:00

If you've never eaten East African cuisine before, you might be surprised to know it's been largely vegan for centuries, owing to the Tewahedo tradition of the faithful abstaining from consuming animal products during fasts, which occur more than twice a week. As a result of this piety and the produce naturally available, today's restaurant menus will reliably have all manner of vegetable stews, with spices in abundance and the region's staple dish, injera (a spongy, sourdough flatbread), to tie everything together. This food is really best for sharing, so if you're with a friend or a few, Keren View is a good place to get your grub on. You can choose sharing dishes for two for under £20 or four for under £40. The space is definitely in the domain of casual dining too, considering injera is typically eaten with the hands, so you can opt to eat in or take away. Enjoying your meal with a few Asmara lagers - the most popular of Eritrean beers - can rarely go amiss.

£
Vegan

Loving Hut 7

Casual Chinese vegan diner
669 Holloway Road, N19 5SE
www.lovinghut.com
Travel: Archway LU
Tue-Fri 12:00-15:00 & 18:00-23:00, Sat-Sun 18:00-23:00

Part of the flourishing vegan scene on Holloway Road, Loving Hut is a worldwide chain, with an Asian-centric menu largely fleshed out with faux meat dishes. It's popular with locals and visiting vegans alike, drawn by a cuisine that traditionally has been inseparable from animal products. This heritage has evidently inspired the menu too - think faux prawn, faux chicken, faux duck - all of which has been fried and battered, and is usually served with glutinous noodles or pancakes and salty sauces.

Their banana or pineapple fritters dusted with cinnamon and icing sugar are our favourite way to wrap up a meal here. The food is tasty, but heavily processed, making for not entirely guilt-free dining. Prices are between £10 to £15 for a meal, making it good value compared with many London alternatives. The interior is charmingly kitsch too, giving the place a down-to-earth vibe. Loving Hut is everything you'd want and expect from a cheap, canteen-style eatery.

£
Vegan

Branch

Neat Burger

Start-up king of sustainable eating
38 Well's Terrace, Finsbury Park, N4 3FP
www.neat-burger.com
For review, see p.50

KING'S CROSS, EUSTON & ISLINGTON

1. The Gate Islington
2. Indian Veg
3. Itadaki Zen
4. Jam Delish
5. Mildred's King's Cross
6. Namaste@OMNOM
7. Tofu Vegan

CALEDONIAN RD
& BARNSBURY
OFFORD RD
THORNHILL RD
BEWDLEY ST
LIVERPOOL ROAD
UPPER ST
ALWYNE VILLAS
ALWYNE RD
CANONBURY GROVE
CANONBURY RD
HALTON RD
ESSEX RD
Barnsbury Wood
Barnsbury Square Garden
BRIDGEMAN RD
LOFTING RD
BARNSBURY ST
Canonbury Gardens
NEW NORTH RD
Thornhill Square
Milner Square
GREENMAN ST
CROSS ST
HEMINGFORD RD
RICHMOND AVE
MATILDA ST
Barnard Park
BARNSBURY RD
CLOUDSLEY RD
Gibson Square
THEBERTON ST
POPHAM ST
ISLINGTON GREEN
COPENHAGEN ST
LIVERPOOL ROAD
COLEBROOKE ROW
ST PETER'S ST
RHEIDOL TERR
UPPER STREET
RODNEY ST
CHAPEL MARKET
DUNCAN ST
NOEL RD
PENTON ST
VINCENT TERR
ANGEL
Joseph Grimaldi Park
GRAHAM ST
CITY RD BASIN
WHARF RD
PENTONVILLE ROAD
CITY ROAD
Myddelton Square
CRUIKSHANK ST
Holford Gardens
GREAT PERCY ST
GOSWELL RD
ST JOHN ST
AMWELL ST
ROSEBERRY AVE
KING'S CROSS RD
1
2
3
4
5
6
7

The Gate Islington ❶

An entry point for ethical eating

370 St John St, EC1V 4NN
020 7833 0401
www.thegaterestaurants.com
Insta: @gaterestaurant
Travel: Angel LU
Tue-Wed 17:00-22:30, Thu-Fri 12:00-22:30,
Sat 10:00-22:30, Sun 10:00-21:30

Located opposite Sadler's Wells Theatre in a spacious Grade II-listed building, The Gate Islington upholds the core values and cooking standards the brand has been renowned for since 1989. The company is now rightly recognised as an institution of fine vegetarian food. The founder's Indian and Iraqi heritage shines through many of the dishes, although you are by no means limited to these fertile regions, for everything from aubergine schnitzel to artichoke gnocchi are also on offer. Feta & couscous fritters, crispy courgette flowers and rosemary salted fries are three other things you'd be foolish not to try. Main meals are priced between £15 and £20, while starters and sides settle for around half as much. The dining space is a refreshingly grown-up environment in comparison to the many Millennial and Gen-Z-oriented outfits cropping up all over London, so do book yourself a table for a special occasion. We recommend you take time over the extensive drinks menu that has everything from mocktails to vegan wines.

£££
Vegan

Branches:

51 Queen Caroline Street, W6 9QL (see p.154)
Marylebone, 22-24 Seymour Place, W1H 7NL (see p.65)

Aloo
Peas

Indian Veg ❷

Great value Indian buffet
92-93 Chapel Market, N1 9EX
020 7837 4607
www.theindianveg.wordpress.com
Insta: @indianveg
Travel: Angel LU
Daily 12:00-22:30

After years of dishing out great value veggie fare, this north London institution has acquired a loyal following and is always popular with local workers looking for a cheap and tasty lunch. Indian Veg offers a simple setting within which to enjoy a freshly prepared array of hearty curries and sides - all self-service as an all-you-can-eat buffet.

You can be sure that all the dishes are vegetarian and they've got vegan options too. It's also great value with £7.95 entitling you to graze until your heart's content and takeaway options cost even less. Humorous posters of vegetarian propaganda line the walls, providing information and jokes on the diet and lifestyle. They claim to be an eco-friendly establishment as well as abstaining from animal products and providing free takeaway food to homeless people in the area. It has a charmingly old-school interior and is BYOB making it one of the best places in Islington if you're looking to eat meat-free.

£
Vegetarian

Itadaki Zen 3

Japanese vegan food

139 King's Cross Road, WC1X 9BJ
020 7278 3573
www.itadakizen-uk.com
Travel: King's Cross LU
Tue-Sat 12:00-14:00 & 17:30-22:00

Japanese and vegan aren't usually two words used in the same sentence, but you can think again with Itadaki Zen. A short walk from King's Cross station, this authentic and unique restaurant stands out from the crowd by offering a cruelty-free alternative to a cuisine that rarely excludes fish or meat of some kind. They've got an exceptionally well-curated array of set menus and sushi dishes to choose from, all of which incorporate essential ingredients like miso, seaweed and yuzu. Everything is presented in the traditional Japanese style we've grown to love. You can choose from classics like shoyu ramen, mochi buns and of course, sushi rolls. Our favourite is the Kansei-han Tanno set - not just for how well it's presented, but also because it's so jam-packed with flavour and good ingredients. The interior complements the food with warm lighting, clay walls and wooden furnishing transporting you straight to Japan. Seating is limited, so booking for the evening is recommended. They have a great lunch deal which includes one main and one side for £14 but if you're visiting in the evening be prepared to spend £20 or more per person for a complete meal. Everything is vegan, organic and prepared to order, so it's worth every penny. In short, come for an unusual vegan take on Japanese cuisine, make sure you book a table and enjoy an evening of culinary adventure in this cosy restaurant.

£££
Vegan

Jam Delish ❹

Jamaican just went vegan again
1 Tolpuddle Street, N1 0XT
0795 7439 777
www.jamdelish.co.uk
Insta: @jam.delish
Travel: Angel LU
Tue-Fri 17:00-22:30, Sat 12:00-22:30, Sun 13:00-19:00

Jam Delish might be only the latest Jamaican restaurant to grace London with its fiery flavours, but that is where the parallels with most other Caribbean eateries end, for they really are one of a kind. The glitz of the interior includes neon-adorned 'living' walls and colourful cocktails which are sure to draw in the influencer crowds. This is complemented by some of the most convincing vegan interpretations of classics like goat curry, jerk barbecue and saltfish you'll find in the capital. And if faux meats aren't your thing, then fear not, for deep-fried buttermilk oyster mushrooms are as delicious as they sound, whilst oxtail-like jackfruit stews are swimming with cassava dumplings dying to be fished out. There are even some playful riffs on food from further afield, like a jerk baba ghanoush and Caribbean-style tacos. Big plates cost just under £20 and small plates settle around £10, so it's more of a sit-down affair than a pop-in while passing by. Jam Delish are a much-welcomed addition to the city's vibrant community of plant-based restaurants.

£££
Vegan

Mildred's King's Cross 5

Ethical international cooking
200 Pentonville Rd, N1 9JP
www.mildreds.co.uk
Insta: @mildredsrestaurants
Travel: Angel LU
Mon-Sat 09:00-23:00, Sun 09:00-22:00

Mildred's has been around since 1988, offering an inspired international take on vegetarian cuisine when so much veggie food at the time was dull and stodgy. This branch has been around for years and offers the usual Mildred's menu including burritos, burgers (try their cannellini apricot patty) alongside South East Asian curries and broths, and many more dishes borrowed from global cuisine. They also have a grown-up selection of drinks, with plenty of organic wines and cocktails from which to choose.

Prices reflect the quality of the food and the ambiance, with mains fixed at £15 and smaller plates for £5 to £8. The Mildred's ethos seems to be popular as they have an ever expanding chain of restaurants across town (see below). One of the longest and most successful plant-focused food establishments in London, Mildred's has a deservedly loyal following.

££
Vegetarian

Branches:
Covent Garden, 79 St Martin's Square, WC2N 4AA
Soho, 45 Lexington Street, W1F 9AN, see p.48
King's Cross, 200 Pentonville Rd, N1 9JP
Camden, 9 Jamestown Rd, NW1 7BW
Dalston, 1 Dalston Square, E8 3GU

Namaste@OMNOM ❻

Enlightened eating

Islington Square, 116N Upper Street, N1 1QP
0730 522 5501
www.omnom.com
Insta: @omnom
Travel: Angel LU
Mon 17:00-22:00, Tue-Sun 12:00-14:30 & 17:00-22:00

If you're in search of an ethical dining experience in London, you'd be hard pressed to find better than Namaste@OMNOM. This innovative collaboration combines ancient principles of both charity and circularity, with a modern approach to restauranting, creating a system whereby each meal served funds another for impoverished children in the developing world. So, you can chow down on a jackfruit biryani, butter masala or some gunpowder potatoes without a care in the world, knowing your cash is going to a good place and that it's all vegetarian or vegan. Mains range between £10 and £15, whilst sides and smaller plates go for around half as much. The OMNOM experience extends beyond just the food, as the dedicated OMSpace above the ground-floor restaurant area hosts a diverse range of events including yoga and mindfulness classes, conferences, corporate training, private parties, and even live comedy performances from comedians like Russell Brand - who is also one of their celebrity ambassadors. And as with the food, for every yoga class attended, a child in a developing country is provided with a hot, healthy, and nutritionally balanced meal. For enlightened eating in the heart of Islington, Namaste@OMNOM is a strong recommendation.

£££
Vegetarian

Tofu Vegan ❼

The go-to vegan Chinese restaurant
105 Upper St, London N1 1QN
www.tofuvegan.com
Insta: @tofuveganlondon
Travel: Angel LU
Mon-Thur 12:00-22:30, Fri-Sat 12:00-22:45, Sun 12:00-21:15

Tofu Vegan have established themselves as the go-to vegan Chinese restaurant. It is rare to find non-westernized Chinese food, but here you are spoilt for choice - with nine different types of dumplings, lotus leaf buns and cucumber salads. As you may have guessed, there is a lot of tofu on the menu, but it's transformed into succulent vegan chicken or sizzling like the most enticing of its pork counterparts. While there are plenty of imitation meats made mostly from bean proteins, there are also simple untranslated dishes like cloud ear fungus salad with coriander and picked chilli or sizzling fried king oyster mushrooms that still affirm vegetables as 'king'. In just two years since opening, Tofu Vegan has already spawned two new branches - a testament to its popularity. While the interiors are kept plain, with wooden countertops and grey leather chairs, the food is transportive. Starters cost around £8 and hot dishes for £12-15. The desserts are for the more adventurous with ingredients like 'sweet bean' and 'lotus seed' paste, which the western palette isn't accustomed to but are absolutely delicious. Tofu Vegan is changing people's perceptions of Chinese food and long may they continue to thrive.

££
Vegan

Branches:
Golders Green, 28 N End Rd, NW11 7PT
Spitalfields, 54 Commercial Street, E1 6LT

DRUMMOND STREET

1. Chutney's
2. Diwana Bhel Poori House
3. Ravi Shankar Bhel Poori

Drummond Street

A hub for South Indian eateries

Chutney's ❶

124 Drummond Street, NW1 2PA; 020 7388 0604
www.chutneysnw1.co.uk; Travel: Euston Square LU;
Mon-Sat 12:00-14:30, 17:00-23:00, Sun 12:00-22:30

Diwana Bhel Poori House ❷

121-123 Drummond Street, NW1 2HL; 020 7387 5556
www.diwanabph.com; Travel: Euston Square LU;
Mon-Sat 12:00-22:30, Sun 12:00-21:30

Ravi Shankar Bhel Poori ❸

133-135 Drummond Street, NW1 2HL; 020 7388 6458
www.ravishankarbhelpoori.com; Travel: Euston Square LU;
Daily 12:00-23:00

Drummond Street is known for its concentration of Indian and Bangladeshi restaurants, all offering great value and delicious food. Three in particular stand out. Diwana Bhel Poori House claims to be the oldest vegetarian South Indian restaurant in London. Here you'll find thalis, dosas and curries aplenty. Chutney's and Ravi Shankar offer similar fare but also have a buffet during lunch times and à la carte in the evenings. Of the three, Diwana has a more extensive menu, but all have vegan options. Vegans should always ask if their dish contains ghee or paneer (butter and curd cheese), which are both found extensively in this cuisine. Tasty meals cost between £5 and £10, making Drummond Street a great place for simple veggie Indian food. Remember to bring your own bottle.

£
Vegetarian

Chutney's

STOKE NEWINGTON

1. Bodega 50
2. Made in Hackney & Food for All
3. The Muddy Puddle
4. Plant Club
5. Rasa
6. Wave

STOKE NEWINGTON
2
CAZENOVE RD
ABNEY PARK CEMETERY
YOAKLEY RD
NORTHWOLD RD
STOKE NEWINGTON CHURCH ST
5
KERSLEY RD
DEFOE RD
DYNEVOR RD
LAWRENCE RD
STOKE NEWINGTON HIGH ST
STOKE NEWINGTON COMMON
RECTORY RD
BROOKE RD
KYNASTON RD
OLDFIELD RD
ALBION RD
LESWIN RD
BAYSTON RD
DYNEVOR RD
VICTORIAN GROVE
RECTORY ROAD
BARBAULD RD
6
EVERING RD
MANSE RD
NEVILL RD
BEATTY RD
AMHURST RD
SYDNER RD
RECTORY RD
3
WALFORD RD
FOULDEN RD
MILTON GROVE
ALLEN RD
BRIGHTON RD
DOWNS RD
HACKNE DOWNS
1
BUTTERFIELD GREEN
PALANTINE RD
FARLEIGH RD
ALBION RD
WORDSWORTH RD
STOKE NEWINGTON HIGH ST
SHACKLEWELL RD
AMHURST RD
PRINCE GEORGE RD
HOWARD RD
PRINCESS MAY RD
BARRETT'S GROVE
MATTHIAS RD
NEWINGTON GREEN

Bodega 50 ❶

Stokey locals' favourite spot
50 Allen Road, N16 8RZ
020 7683 3869
Insta: @bodega50
Travel: Rectory Road LO
Daily 08:00-16:00

Bodega – the Spanish word used for local grocery stores in New York – is a fitting name for this neighbourhood café that satisfies the vegetarian dining needs of the Stoke Newington crowd. Tucked away from the main road, Bodega 50 remains a little-known gem that is treasured by its local patrons who come to enjoy the comforting food, coffee and relaxed atmosphere.

Simple lunch dishes like sourdough toasties, salads and soups are made fresh and priced low, which keeps it all just as sweet as the great pastries on offer. You won't be disappointed by their oat milk lattes either – they do full justice to the artisan coffee beans. In fact, the only things that aren't vegan are croissants and the occasional pastry, but just ask before you buy if you have any doubts.

The space inside has a cool Scandi vibe and is a good place to eat with kids. Bodega 50 also has its own in-café dog called Bruce who is very amicable. You can enjoy a light breakfast or lunch and drink here for as little as £5. This little café might be hard to find but it is definitely one to seek out when visiting Stokey.

£
Vegetarian

Branch:
442 Hoe Street, E17 9AH

BO
DE
GA
50
BELU

Made in Hackney & Food for All ❷

3 Cazenove Road, N16 6PA
020 8442 4266 & 020 8806 4138
www.madeinhackney.org & www.foodforall.co.uk
Travel: Stoke Newington LO
Made in Hackney open for consultation/classes only
Food For All: Mon-Fri 9:00-18:00, Sat 22:00-18:00,
Sun 11:00-16:30

Made in Hackney is the kind of community initiative every borough needs. It's a kitchen and cookery school that runs regular courses and classes on how to live better, sharing personal, hands-on experiences of healthy vegan eating with thousands of people every year. One of the team's ambassadors is Dr Rupy Aujla, who teaches the UK's first culinary medicine course at Bristol University. The team also boasts professional chefs, activists and community workers. Classes range from growing food in urban environments to cooking vegan junk food, while courses aim to teach skills that will establish a lifetime of plant-based cooking. Much of this is free or on a pay-by-donation basis. Made in Hackney also works with schools, charities and housing associations.

If you need the ingredients to start a plant-based diet, Food For All is based at the entrance and is a health food shop that's been providing Hackney residents with vegetarian and vegan health products for over 40 years. Here you'll find locally made shea butter, herbal remedies, alongside affordable, high-quality wholefoods. They too have many links to humanitarian causes, particularly with AMURT, a charity that focuses on community development and disaster relief. Made in Hackney and Food For All are ethical, independent and not-for-profit organisations that deserve your support.

The Muddy Puddle ❸

Ethical empanadas
142 Albion Road, N16 9PA
020 7052 4080
www.the-muddy-puddle.business.site
Insta: @themuddy_puddle
Travel: Rectory Road LO
Tue-Thur 08:00-16:00, Fri 08:00-22:00, Sat 09:00-17:00, Sun 10:00-17:00

South American food is one of the less frequently encountered options on our high streets. But a change in the weather is coming, evident in the arrival of The Muddy Puddle. This ethical eatery, run by an Argentinian, is offering up established favourites like empanadas, alongside reinterpreted classics like the Full English (which comes with spicy chickpeas and fried polenta). Other enticing options include burritos and a wide selection of natural wines, but coffee is expectedly their strong suit. Pair this perfectly with banana and chia pudding, or amazing pastries like pretzel blondies and choux buns, and you won't be disappointed. Their space is comfy and includes a great (covered) garden area for when the weather is right. With breakfasts between £8 and £13, it's just about in line with local prices, so you needn't pay a premium to eat plant-based when passing through.

£-££
Vegan

Plant Club ❹

Cooking by Britain's 'Pasta Chef of the Year'

49 Green Lanes, N16 9BU
07888 295 517
www.plantclub.uk
Insta: @plant_clubuk
Travel: Canonbury LO
Thur-Fri 17:00-22:00, Sat 13:00-23:00, Sun 13:00-20:00

This is a review that (almost) writes itself. Antonio Alderuccio's recent crowning as Britain's 'best pasta chef of the year' - with a menu from his vegan and gluten-free establishment - is a seismic event in matters of Italian food and the London restaurants that serve it. You too can try the paccheri that earned him this hallowed position, which comes coated in a courgette sauce, with asparagus, Burella (a vegan burrata alternative) and breadcrumbs. Or else, their arancini, truffle gnocchi or bolognese - all of which are cooked and served with some of the finest dairy-free cheeses. And that other hallmark of Italian cuisine - pizza - is the next project Alderuccio is undertaking with his signature gluten-free & plant-based style. Everything from Margherita to calzone is covered, with ingredients like Vesuvian tomatoes given pride of place. With priced between £12 and £17 for a main, and half of that for starters and desserts, as well as bottles of wine from £28, Plant Club will by no means break the bank despite its pedigree, so do pencil in a time to book a table.

££
Vegan

Rasa 5

Colourful Keralan cuisine
55 Stoke Newington Church Street, N16 0AR
020 7249 0344
www.rasarestaurants.com
Insta: @rasarestaurants
Travel: Stoke Newington LO
Tue-Fri 17:30-22:30, Sat & Sun 12:00-14:30, 17:30-22:30

Think pink when you think Rasa – this Keralan restaurant stands out not only for its curries, but also for the eye-catching hue of its façade. This long-standing Stoke Newington institution has gained a reputation for serving unique and fresh vegetarian curries. The mixed curry platters served on a steel tray are a good way to sample this style of South Indian cuisine, and specials like mango curries are worth a try. You really can find all the colours of the rainbow in Rasa's food, with beets and bananas among the extensive list of tropical fruits, vegetables and spices at play in their dishes. As always, rice and bread (including the less common appam - a crispy rice pancake) accompany these curries perfectly. There's plenty of vegan fare and the dishes not containing ghee or paneer are clearly labelled. You'll likely total around £10 for a good meal here. It's always worth trying to book in advance, as Rasa are popular, but it repays the effort as this is one of north London's best veggie Indian restaurants.

£-££
Vegetarian

Branch

Wave

Minimalist interiors meet maximalist ingredients
1A Evering Road, Stoke Newington, N16 7AH
www.weareveganeverything
For review, see p.287

WEST

Holy Carrot p.158

FULHAM

222 Vegan Cuisine

Eclectic international eatery
222 North End Road, W14 9NU
020 7381 2322
www.222vegancuisine.com
Insta: @222vegancuisine
Travel: West Kensington LU, West Brompton LO
Daily 12:00-21:00

222 Vegan Cuisine is a popular restaurant that's been serving low-fat, low-salt, non-GM, plant-based food since 2004. But don't let all that jargon put you off, for the food is hearty and plentiful. This cosy neighbourhood eatery makes for a great casual lunch out or a more formal dinner. The menu plucks the best and most veggie-adaptable dishes from around the globe, including Egusi from West Africa, Russian Seitan Stroganoff and Oyster Mushroom & Spinach Raclette from Switzerland. But our firm favourite is their Spaghetti Polpette, with meatballs made from quinoa and spinach. Mains all cost around £12 and their starters around £6, which considering their dishes are made from almost entirely organic produce, is great value. Desserts are where they really shine and their vegan nut-based cheesecake won't disappoint.

Head chef, Ben Asamani, has established quite a reputation and for an evening meal, it's advisable to book in advance. With careful lighting, a subtle soundtrack and attentive service, the effort will be rewarded with one of the best vegan dining experiences to be found in the capital.

££-£££
Vegan

HAMMERSMITH

The Gate

International fine dining
51 Queen Caroline Street, W6 9QL
020 8748 6932
www.thegaterestaurants.com
Insta: @gaterestaurant
Travel: Hammersmith LU
Mon-Wed 17:00-22.30, Thur-Fri 12:00-14:30 & 17:00-22:30, Sat 12:00-16:00 & 17:00-22:30, Sun 12:00-16:00 & 17:00-21:30

With a reputation spanning 30 years, The Gate has earned itself the right to call itself a vegetarian institution. It aims to offer a gourmet meat-free dining experience across its three branches, by way of attractively presented global cuisine served within their fashionably designed spaces. The international menu features diverse dishes, but though you might find the odd curry or schnitzel, French and Italian food predominate. In particular, we're big fans of the Rotolo. The flavours are adventurous, showing that vegetarian (and vegan) food can be bold, and the presentation is artful without scrimping on portions.

They also serve a host of great beers, wines and cocktails, giving a grown-up appeal to the experience here. The three branches can be characterised as 'modern chic', with high ceilings, sleek furniture and carefully designed lighting. The mains cost on average £16, with separate courses, sides and drinks for less, so a three-course meal will likely cap at £40 per person. During the festive season, they offer an incredible set menu for around the £40 mark which is great value. As happens with chains, you don't get the same sense of individuality within each branch as you might with an independent, but The Gate still offers a rarely paralleled quality of food and service for vegans and vegetarians in London.

£££
Vegetarian

Branches:

Marylebone, 22-24 Seymour Place, W1H 7NL (see p.65)
Islington, 370 St John St, EC1V 4N (see p.120)

Branch

Sagar

South Indian

157 King Street, W6 9JT

www.sagarveg.co.uk

For review, see p.53

KENSINGTON & CHELSEA

1. Holy Carrot
2. Juicebaby
3. Mali Vegan Thai
4. Raw Press
5. Wulf and Lamb

HANS RD
CHEVAL PL
BROMPTON SQUARE
BEAUCHAMP PL
Hans Place Garden
BROMPTON RD
YEOMAN'S ROW
PONT ST
THURLOE PL
EGERTON GRDNS
BROMPTON RD
Lennox Gardens
CADOGAN SQ
CADOGAN SQ
PAVILION RD
SLOANE ST
CADOGEN PL
CADOGEN LANE
WALTON ST
MILNER ST
CADOGEN PL
ELLIS ST
PAVILION RD
SLOANE TERR
PELHAM ST
Pelham Crescent
FULHAM RD
LUCAN PL
SLOANE AVE
DRAYCOTT AVE
CADOGAN ST
CADOGAN GRDNS
SYMONS ST
SLOANE SQUARE
POND PL
IXWORTH PL
ELYSTAN ST
WHITEHEAD'S GROVE
DRAYCOTT PL
KING'S RD
CHELSEA BRIDGE
HOLBEIN PL
Saatchi Gallery
CALE ST
ELYSTAN PLACE
BRITTEN ST
KING'S RD
SMITH ST
ST LEONARD'S TER
TURK'S ROW
ROYAL HOSPITAL RD
Burton Court
1
2
3
4
5

Holy Carrot ❶

Taking vegetables to higher planes

Urban Retreat, 2-4 Hans Crescent, SW1X 0LH
020 3897 0404
www.holycarrot.co.uk
Insta: @holycarrotrestaurant
Travel: Knightsbridge LU
Mon-Sat 12:00-22:00, Sun 11:00-17:00

There are two types of vegans in this world: quinoa-chomping plant lovers, and those who once enjoyed meat but think the lives of the planet and its creatures are more important. For anyone who falls into the latter category, Holy Carrot is the spot for you. It's nestled within the Urban Retreat complex, a beauty salon operating from Knightsbridge's very own White House - a magnificent former aristocrat's mansion, bathed in natural light and exuding an undeniable air of grandeur. Inside, you'll find ethically sourced seasonal fare with delightful vegan substitutes, such as the ingenious seafood platter - which includes hearts of palm calamari-style, faux tuna and scallop maki, and convincing crab croquettes, as well as shepherd's pie made with tempeh and black lentils. Their afternoon tea is a work of art, with the sweet treats including miso and caramel sponge cake and pistachio éclair and savoury offerings such as croquettes and crostini. At £40 per person, it blows the local competition of luxury hotels out of the water. If you fancy lunch or dinner then small plates are around £10, and larger ones just under £20.

£££
Vegan

Branch

Juicebaby ❷

Vegan, gluten-free and raw café
398 King's Road, SW10 0LJ
www.juicebaby.co.uk
For review, see p.172

Mali Vegan Thai

Mali Vegan Thai ❸

London's first 100% vegan Thai
5a Hogarth Place, SW5 0QT
0749 418 3205
www.malivegan.co.uk
Insta: @mali.vegan
Travel: Earl's Court LU
Wed-Sun 12:00-15:00 & 17:30-22:00, Tue 17:30-22:00

In recent years Thai food has flourished in Britain's restaurant scene. Some of the most popular restaurants in the capital, both luxury and quotidian, are serving up spicy laabs and sumptuous massamans for an ever-increasing supply of hungry punters. But as is often the case, this has been a meaty affair, so fast-forward to the launch of Mali Vegan Thai, and we have London's first fully vegan restaurant on our hands. However, you needn't give up your favourite dishes, for Mali's clever use of omni meats has meant you can still chow down on mince, chicken and fish dishes, whilst classic curries, stir-fries and salads come chock full of vibrant veg and spice. Pride of place goes to the fresh pea flowers and vegetable rolls, or else their kanom pang na moo, a kind of Thai bruschetta. Small plates range between £5 and £9, whereas larger dishes like tom yum or pad thai cost £11 to £16. Mali is a more sit-down affair, but you'll get a choice of both indoor and outdoor seating.

££
Vegan

Raw Press ❹

Vegan, gluten-free and raw café
3 Ellis Street, SW1X 9AL
020 7730 4347
www.rawpress.co
Insta: @rawpress.co
Travel: Sloane Square LU
Mon-Fri 08:00-19:00, Sat-Sun 09:00-19:00

Raw Press has been at the forefront of the UK's raw food movement and specialises in cold-pressed juices. They proselytise this food preparation technique for both its health benefits and improved flavours and have a following of subscribers to their juice cleanse care packages. These are a great way to get closer to your 5-a-day but, visiting the café, the food is very much to the fore.

Serving sweet and savoury dishes, salads and a couple of hot dishes throughout the day, the food here is colourful, healthy and freshly prepared. A must-try is the Instagram-worthy blueberries and buckwheat waffle, not least because it feels like an indulgence without having any naughty ingredients to worry about. Free Wi-Fi and an inviting interior make this a great spot to convert into your impromptu office for an hour or two, but it's also a good place for a healthy break while shopping in the West End. Raw Press also offers a fantastic buffet service which is healthy and satisfying but comes at a fairly high price considering this is more a café than a restaurant. For those committed to a raw, vegan and gluten-free diet, this is a great central London café and one well worth trying. Once you've tried their chia bowl with a green juice, chances are you'll be back for more.

££
Vegan
Gluten-free
Raw

SOUP
NACHO PLATTER
SMALL SALAD
REGULAR SALAD
SALADS ARE VEGAN
AND GLUTEN FREE
COFFEES AND TEAS
SELECTION AVAILABLE
FROM VOLCANO COFFEE
& RARE TEA COMPANY
COLD DRINKS

Wulf and Lamb 5

No predators, no prey
243 Pavilion Road, SW1X 0BP
020 3948 5999
www.wulfandlamb.com
Insta: @wulfandlamb
Travel: Sloane Square LU
Sun-Thur 09:00-21:00, Fri & Sat 09:00-22:00

Wulf and Lamb offers a chic vegan dining experience, as befits its salubrious Chelsea location. Found among a hub of shops and eateries on Pavilion Road, it serves global cuisine in a smartly designed but comfortable interior with outside seating at the front and a wonderful lush dining area to the rear which is perfect on fine days. Burgers, curry, chilli and pie can all be enjoyed here, or you can just opt for their delicious range of coffee and puddings.

Wulf and Lamb use locally sourced and organic produce wherever possible, some of which comes from Natoora down the road. They are more expensive than a lot of vegan eateries, with burgers and most other mains costing in the vicinity of £15, and sides and snacks costing between £4 and £9. They make up for the cost with plentiful portions, which have made this a popular eatery with locals and passing tourists. The food won't leave you feeling guilty, but perhaps the bill will, so Wulf and Lamb are best saved for a cruelty-free treat.

££-£££
Vegan

Branch:
66 Chiltern Street, W1U 4EJ, Tel: 020 8194 0000

NOTTING HILL

❶ Clean Kitchen
❷ Farmacy
❸ Juicebaby
❹ Portobello Health Foods

Shops:

A) Eden Perfumes, see p.325
B) Planet Organic see p.327
C) Portobello Wholefoods, see p.328

WESTBOURNE PARK
WESTWAY
ACKLAM RD
TAVISTOCK RD
CAMBRIDGE GRDNS
LADBROKE GROVE
LANCASTER RD
PORTOBELLO RD
BASING ST
WESTBOURNE PARK RD
TALBOT RD
CHEPSTOW RD
HEREFORD RD
NEWTON RD
LEDBURY RD
ARTESIAN RD
COLVILLE TERRACE
BLENHEIM CRESCENT
LONSDALE RD
WESTBOURNE GROVE
CHEPSTOW PL
LEINSTER SQUARE
ELGIN CRESCENT
KENSINGTON PARK RD
CHEPSTOW VILLAS
PEMBRIDGE CRES
PEMBRIDGE RD
DAWSON PL
PEMBRIDGE SQUARE
MOSCOW RD
LANSDOWNE RD
LADBROKE SQUARE
NOTTING HILL GATE
BAYSWATER RD
LADBROKE RD

Clean Kitchen ❶

Chain store by Made in Chelsea crew
172 Portobello Road, W11 2EB
www.cleankitchen.club
Insta: @cleankitchenuk
Travel: Notting Hill Gate LU
Mon-Sun 08:00-22:00

For witnesses to London's vegan restaurant scene emergence over the last few years, Clean Kitchen will be very familiar. Their menu takes a tour of the staples of a plant-based menu - smoothies, acai and salad bowls, burgers, basically as much faux meat as you can eat between two pieces of bread. This is fast food after all. They've explicitly stated their aim is to become the 'plant-based McDonald's' - so expect all manner of fries, nuggets and desserts like cheesecake too. But as their name suggests, 'cleanliness' runs through this all, from the sustainability of their ingredients and into the dining space with its simple modern interior. In truth, it might be a while until they dethrone the cheapest of fast food chains, with all their burgers costing close to £10 and sides around half of that. But then again, you don't get luxuries like truffle mayo or smoked 'salmon' there, so stop by and give them a try to see for yourself.

£-££
Vegan

Branches:
64 Old Compton Street, W1D 4UQ
198 Camden High Street, NW1 8QP
Boxpark Wembley, Wembley Park, HA9 0JT

TRIP
TRIP

Farmacy ❷

Where food becomes medicine
74 Westbourne Grove, W2 5SH
020 7221 0705
www.farmacylondon.com
Insta: @farmacyuk
Travel: Bayswater & Royal Oak LU
Mon-Thur 12:00-22:00, Fri 11:00-22:00, Sat & Sun 10:00-22:00

Farmacy certainly has the look and feel of the kind of classy, high-end restaurant that you would expect in this neck of the woods. The rustic tables and chic minimalist chairs wrap around a 360 degrees bar, and the whole space is teeming with lush plant life. But this botanic interior isn't just an empty aesthetic, all food served here is 100% organic with much of the produce harvested from their farm in Kent. The menu is full of on-trend dishes that make use of superfoods like tigernut milk and probiotics. They offer bowls, burgers and breakfasts too, presented attractively, but in small portions. These come with a higher price tag than you will pay at other places, with their signature 'Farmacy Benedict' (served with GF waffles) costing £17. Their puddings and pancakes satisfy all those sweet cravings while being free of dairy, refined sugars and additives, and their showstopper Brownie Sundae (£13.50) is uncharacteristically substantial. A filling breakfast will likely set you back £20, and if you're dining here in the evening and drink alcohol, then expect to set aside at least £50 per person. Farmacy may be expensive, but they do offer a welcome opportunity for vegans to enjoy luxury dining.

£££
Vegan

Juicebaby ❸

Vegan, gluten-free and raw café
181 Westbourne Grove, W11 2SB
020 7221 2144
www.juicebaby.co.uk
Insta: @juicebabyuk
Travel: Notting Hill Gate LU
Mon-Fri 07:30-19:00, Sat 08:00-19:00, Sun 08:00-18:00

Juicebaby is a welcome addition to west London high streets, offering a healthy, vegan, 'clean-eating' kitchen with plenty of takeout options. Their philosophy is all about substituting the bad for the deceptively good, and they've pulled it off with their organic juices, salad bowls, acai and sweet treats. This is the place to eat if you want to feel naughty but not nasty, as their goods are all carefully made, as unprocessed as possible and without any of those troublesome ingredients - gluten, refined sugars and chemical preservatives. The shops are both laid out similarly, with lots of comfy benches and tables to enjoy your food. Prices are especially reasonable for a clean-eating Kensington eatery. You can expect to slurp or munch down a meal here for around £13, with most lunch options costing around £9, and drinks and snacks for less. Juicebaby is a good option if you're looking for healthy food in a fashionable but relaxed atmosphere.

££
Vegan
Raw

Branch at:
398 Kings Road, SW10 0LJ

ORGANIC

Portobello Health Foods ❹

Perennial part of Portobello

269A Portobello Road, W11 1LR
020 7229 5571
Insta: @portobellohealthfood
Travel: Ladbroke Grove LU
Mon-Sun 10:00-20:00

If you're just looking for some healthy, tasty, no-frills fare, then look no further than Portobello Health Foods. Since 1971, they've dished up all manner of meat-free favourites, from curries and stews to salads and pasta bakes, as well as an array of sweet treats. There are over 40 dishes to chose from and many locals queue up for their great value family boxes which will feed a hungry family for just £15.

The interior is a little sparse in the way of seating, with just a few stools and a countertop, so this is best enjoyed as a takeaway option when passing through this part of town. A box of mixed-and-matched costs between £6 and £8, which is easily more than one person is likely to eat in a sitting. If you want more, little extras like a slice of quiche or cake are only £2 to £3 more. There really is no better value veggie food to be found in the capital and all the dishes are prepared freshly each day in their kitchen. When you're next in Portobello, join the locals in the know, and grab yourself a delicious veggie bargain.

£
Vegetarian

RICHMOND

1. Hollyhock Café
2. Tide Tables Café

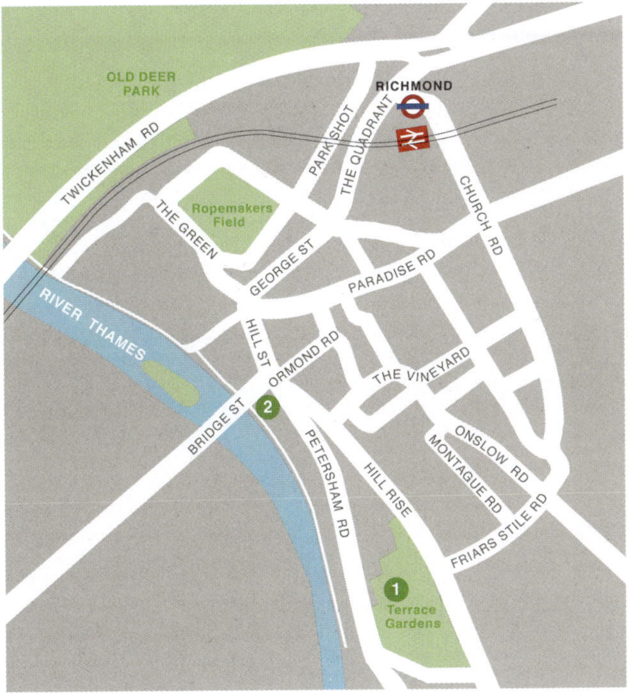

Hollyhock Café ❶

Charming park café
Terrace Gardens, TW10 6UX
020 8948 6555
Travel: Richmond LU/LO
Daily 8:00-17:00

Tide Tables ❷

Homemade café staples
2 The Arches, TW9 1TH
020 8948 8285
www.tidetablescafe.co.uk
Insta: @tidetablescafé
Daily 07:30-17:00

These sister cafés in Richmond are charming spots to enjoy vegetarian food with a view. You can choose between looking onto the river from a large, tree-covered outdoor space and archway, or in a rustic cottage surrounded by the Terrace Gardens. Both serve homely vegetarian and vegan food like pies, lasagne and salad, and only make use of fair trade and organic produce. If you just want a snack they also have a range of beers, hot drinks and pastries. Prices are very fair, with filling mains costing around £5 to £6, and lighter options for a lot less. Though on the outskirts of London, these cafés merit a visit because of their idyllic locations in Richmond, and are surrounded by plenty of things to do and see while there too.

£
Vegetarian

Tide Tables

SOUTH

BRIXTON

1. Alkaline
2. Blank Coffee
3. Eat of Eden
4. Eat of Eden Clapham
5. En Root Clapham
6. Halo Burger
7. KATAKATA
8. Light of Africa
9. Oowee Vegan Brixton
10. Oracles Organic
11. Peachy Goat
12. PIPOCA
13. Temple of Seitan
14. VSource

CLAPHAM HIGH ST
ATHERTON RD
LANDOR RD
HUBERT GROVE
WILLINGTON RD
HARGWYNE ST
COMBERMER RD
STOCKWELL RD
BRIXTON RD
VILLA RD
Max Roach Park
WILTSHIRE RD
GRESHAM RD
CLAPHAM NORTH
PULROSS RD
BRIXTON
BRIXTON
BEDFORD RD
FERNDALE RD
FERNDALE RD
ATLANTIC RD
Brixton Village
SANDMERE RD
ELECTRIC AV
COLDHARBOUR LANE
SOLON RD
BALLATER RD
SANTLEY ST
BRIGHTON TER
KEPLER RD
RAILTON RD
SALTOUN RD
KELLET RD
MERVAN RD
ACRE LANE
BAYTREE RD
STRATHLEVEN RD
BRANKSOME RD
SUDBOURNE RD
BRIXTON HILL
RATTRAY AD
DALBERG RD
HAYTER RD
LYHAM RD
BONHAM RD
ST MATTHEW'S RD
EFRA RD
HORSFORD RD
TRENT RD
MORVAL RD
DULWICH RD
LAMBERT RD
GLANVILLE RD
BRIXTON WATER LN
RAMILLIES CL
JOSEPHINE AVE
ARODENE RD
APPACH RD
BROCKWELL PARK
LYHAM RD
Windmill Gardens
FAIRMOUNT RD
WATERWORKS RD
BEECHDALE RD
JEBB AVE
BRIXTON HILL
ENDYMION RD
HELIX RD
LEANDER RD
TULSE HILL
ELM PARK

Alkaline Brixton ❶

Caribbean juice bar and café
100b Brixton Hill SW2 1AH
020 8678 6900
Insta: @alkalinecleanse
Travel: Brixton LU
Mon-Fri 08:30-15:00, Sat 09:30-16:30

This teeny little spot might be discreetly wedged onto a corner of Brixton Hill, but if passing by it's not one to miss. Alkaline is a juice bar and café that serves juices and street food meals with the finest of vegan, organic produce. With unusual ingredients like bluggoe, burdock, fonio and cacao, there is some serious plant-based power and vitality in Alkaline's goodies.

Salad boxes, raw cakes and stews can all be enjoyed alongside the plethora of drinks on offer. Most things cost between £3 and £5, making this an affordable place to eat, particularly versus the other 'clean-eating' restaurants to be found out West. You might have to compete over the narrow counters and stools, but most of the local health-conscious crowd who make a regular pilgrimage through Alkaline's doors are using the takeaway service. Alkaline has acquired something of a reputation in Brixton and there are often queues, but their fresh juices are worth the wait.

£
Vegan

PATTA

blank.
brixton
144

Blank Coffee ❷

Hidden vegetarian hotspot
144 Acre Lane, SW2 5UT
07736 808 363
Insta: @blankbrixton
Travel: Brixton LU/Clapham North LU
Mon-Fri 07:30-15:00, Sat 07:30-15:30, Sun 08:00-15:30

Just a few years ago, London's veggie and vegan scene was going through its teething phase, with an initial explosion of eateries – the aesthetic was bold, their cruelty-free status worn on their sleeves. Blank Coffee is interesting in that it lets the visitor fill in the blanks, no pun intended. With its aloof monochrome aesthetic, it's discrete about its vegetarianism. This is a trend popular in cities that haven't exactly welcomed the lifestyle with open arms (like Milan), but this is more likely a different impulse, one that wants to normalize vegetarian eateries without having to state it.

While Blank was originally vegan, it introduced cow's milk onto its menu recently but bearing that in mind, its menu is still largely vegan. The food here is very good with café affogato's oozing ice cream over the brim of the glass and meatless sausage rolls that offer a substantial snack. Of course, you can always opt for a healthy vegan scramble of mushrooms, tomatoes and avocado and a regular coffee.

If the good food isn't enough, they also offer yoga classes, a play area for kids and film screenings in their basement. Exposed brick walls, pendant lighting and smooth wooden furnishings give a trendy touch to this down-to-earth spot, where an artisanal coffee costs just £2.50 and meals between £5 and £7. Blank may be a little off the main Brixton drag, but it's worth seeking out.

£
Vegetarian

Eat of Eden ❸

Vegan Caribbean in Brixton Market
Unit 4, Brixton Village, Coldharbour Lane, SW9 8PR
020 7737 7566
www.eatofeden.store
Insta: @eatofeden
Travel: Brixton LU
Daily 11:00-21:00

Brixton has been a home for vegan and vegetarian restaurants owing to its long-standing Caribbean community and their ties to Ital food culture – a Rastafari tradition that eschews consumption of animal products. A walk down Electric Avenue will show you all manner of options to eat, but if you're after an introduction to this cuisine then look no further than Eat of Eden. Its bright green façade is hard to miss, whilst inside await platters of ackee, callaloo, dumplings, plantain, mac pie and much more. If a platter proves too much, patties make for a perfect meal in passing, especially when paired with a reviving juice or smoothie packed full of fruits and powders like sea moss or ashwagandha. Pineapple crumble is an unusual fusion of two different cuisines, but like Brixton's cultural mix, it seems to work. They have a small amount of both indoor and outdoor seating, and you can eat for under £10, but to try a few different things you'll be best served by their platters for £14. For many, Eat of Eden will be a little slice of paradise.

££
Vegan

Branch

Eat of Eden Clapham ❹

Caribbean vegan
Ascot Parade 6, Clapham Park Road, SW4 7EY
www.eatofeden.store

EL RANCHO DE

En Root Clapham ❺

Old-school fare for a brand new crowd

5 Ascot Parade, Clapham Park Road, SW4 7EY
www.enrootldn.co.uk
Insta: @enrootldn
Travel: Clapham North LU
Daily 12:00-21:00

Despite being relatively new to the vegan scene, most plant-based people will recognise there's something of the old-school charm to En Root, who dish up Indian-inspired health food from their colourfully-fronted shops in South London. Expect to see a lot of lentil curries dished up in thalis, alongside some more interesting options like jerk plantain mushrooms and cassava chips, as well as an array of great drinks and desserts packed full of vitalising ingredients like sea moss, cacao and acai. And prices harken back to older times too with small plates costing around £5 and big platters aren't more than £12. They're a tad limited on the seating front, so do get in there before the rest. If you want to take the flavour of En Root on your route home, their award-winning Raja Bonnet hot sauce and Rajanaise will spice up your cooking.

£-££
Vegan

Halo Burger 6

Brixton's blessed burgers

Pop Brixton, 49 Brixton Station Road, SW9 8PQ
www.haloburger.co.uk
Insta: @haloburgeruk
Travel: Brixton LU
Daily 12:00-22:30

Forget the golden arches, for a golden ring floats above the head of anyone eating these burgers, which are as close to a Big Mac as any vegan may come, without the ethical self-sabotage. Halo Burger have even made a vegan sausage and egg muffin, which will satisfy any vegan's desire for a hearty breakfast snack. Loaded fries, onion strips and nuggets are all on offer too, best washed down with a shake or some soft-serve ice cream, for when you're really craving junk food. There isn't an awful lot by way of seating, so this food is perhaps best eaten on the go. They don't quite beat the insanely cheap fast-food prices we've gotten used to as a nation, but are more in line with their more upmarket counterparts, with burgers mostly around the £10 mark, and sides and treats for less than half that. Halo Burger are nonetheless a delicious vegan treat when visiting Brixton and strongly recommended.

£-££
Vegan

STAY FOCUSED
STAY FOCUSED
KATAKATA

KATAKATA ❼

French galettes and crêpes
132 Brixton Hill, SW2 1RS
020 3490 1160
www.katakatabrixton.com
Insta: @katakatabrixton
Travel: Brixton LU
Daily 10:00-22:00

A cheap eat can always be found at KATAKATA. It's a vegetarian café with plenty of vegan options, situated among several salt-of-the-earth eateries that represent what Brixton is all about. Alongside the workshops they run on healthy living and the art and music events they host, you can enjoy French galettes, crêpes and fresh juices here for a lot cheaper than most of the chain restaurants down the road.

Choose between cheesy buckwheat pancakes or vegan alternatives, and fill up with jerk tofu and a tonne of veg too. All galettes come with a carrot, bean shoot, beetroot and spinach salad that is both tasty and filling. A juice and galette combo is just £10, so ditch the supermarket meal deal and get yourself some real food.

£
Vegetarian

Light of Africa ❽

No-frills East African

Unit 55, Brixton Village Market,
Coldharbour Lane, SW9 8PS
07841 449 941
Insta: @lightofafrica55
Travel: Brixton LU
Mon 11:00-18:00, Tue-Sat 11:00-22:30

Light of Africa serves up no-frills Eritrean and Ethiopian fare in and amongst the hustle and bustle of Brixton Village Market. Think injera – the sourdough teff flatbread typical of this East African cuisine – served alongside stews made of okra, pulses, spinach, and pumpkin, as well as all manner of herbs and spices. They've also got a great selection of authentic Ethiopian beers, so if you're looking to try something new then this is the place to go. A platter for one costs £14 and for two £27, making this appear a little more on the expensive side for simple cooking, but if you get through one of these in a sitting you're unlikely to need to eat for most of the rest of the day. Located inside the Brixton Village Market, there's covered outdoor seating with traditional seats that are perfectly shaped to hold a platter, as well as indoor seating. The outdoor seating providing an unparalleled people-watching opportunity while enjoying a taste of Africa.

£-££
Vegan

OOWEE
CONDENSED
DIRTY
SAUCE

Oowee Vegan Brixton ⑨

Food so good it makes you say...
Brixton Village, Unit 91-92, SW9 8PR
020 7274 0321
www.ooweevegan.com
Insta: @oowee_vegan
Travel: Brixton LU
Sun-Wed 11:30-22:30, Thur-Sat 11:30-23:00

This one is for the cheat days, and the indulgence of all those meaty desires you may have been avoiding. Think big ol' beef burgers, stacked chick'n burgers, even more fried chick'n, sides like dirty fries loaded with cheese and jalapenos, or other bits and bobs like tater tots, mac n' cheese, onion rings plus shakes or beer depending on your stripe. Their faux fish range has expanded too, including classic fish and chips and an ocean burger. These are meat substitutes at their best, which is why it's little wonder people have been ooweeing up and down the country - they've now got two branches in both London and Bristol, plus another in Brighton. And you can hardly blame them - burgers only cost between £5 and £10, sides and drinks for around half as much. This means you can expect to eat well for around the same cost as almost any of the other high-street fast-food chains, without the ethical hangup. However they've got limited covered seating available, so you should perhaps best consider Oowee as a takeaway spot par excellence..

£-££
Vegan

Branch:
50 Stoke Newington Road, N16 7XB (see p.265)

Oracles Organic ⑩

Visionary vegan juices and food
Unit 90, Granville Arcade,
Brixton Village, Coldharbour Lane, SW9 8PR
0758 424 0909
www.oraclesorganics.com
Travel: Brixton LU
Sun-Wed 11:00-19:00, Thur-Sat 10:00-22:00

This Jamaican juice bar and vegan eatery is a good option when on the prowl for healthy, organic fare in Brixton. They promote a raw food diet and offer a range of vegetable and fruit juices, so this is the place to come for a shot or two of your five a day, and they make colourful salads, soups and inventive raw dishes like spiral 'spaghetti' too. They also double as a small organic vegan grocer, stocking mostly dry goods as well as probiotics and fresh coconuts. If eating in, then expect to spend around £5 on juices, £5 on soup or £7-10 on their mains, with things costing a little less to take out. There are a few tables and chairs, both inside and outside the store, and you'll always be under the cover of the Brixton Village roof. Oracles Organic is one of the best, healthiest and purely vegan options in the area, and a must-visit for locals.

£
Vegan

IFA

Peachy Goat ⓫

Italian-inspired ethical indulgences

16 Half Moon Lane, SE24 9HU
020 7967 7386
www.peachygoat.com
Insta: @peachygoatldn
Travel: Herne Hill Rail
Tue-Fri 18:00-22:30, Sat & Sun 12:00-15:30 & 18:00-11:00

This is a restaurant that will not disappoint. Really good vegan Italian food has long been just out of reach for plant-based pasta addicts, but that's all beginning to change in the capital, not least because of Peachy Goat.

The menu is, like the name, admittedly a bit of a hodge-podge, with 'Italian-inspired' stretched to include padron peppers, 'camembert bites', and burgers, but if you stick to some classics like orecchiette ragu or 'nduja arancini you can't go wrong. Small plates cost £5-£10, whilst mains cost around £16, making this more on the expensive side of options in the wider Herne Hill area, but this is made up for in quality. With a cosy indoor dining area and some outdoor seating, this is as good for a date spot as for a casual lunch, especially if you need food as good-looking as your company.

££
Vegan

PIPOCA ⓬

Zero-waste vegan store and café
224 Brixton Road, SW9 6AH
020 7501 8539
www.pipocavegan.com
Insta: @pipocavegan
Travel: Brixton LU
Tue-Sat 10:00-20:00, Sun 10:00-17:00

Pipoca began life as a zero-waste store and has since expanded to provide food and coffee as well, doubling up as a café should you be in need of a pitstop. As a stockist of cereals, condiments, drinks, substitutes, cosmetics and much more, almost all your vegan essentials are stocked, as well as those extra niceties for when you want to treat yourself. Plant-based frozen pizzas, freshly baked sourdough, craft beers, and artisan nut spreads are just some of the things to get distracted by on a shop here.

Once you've got your essentials you can cut back and enjoy all that their café has to offer including the Mexican Breakfast, soups that are made daily or delicious turmeric cassava chips. Prices are surprisingly reasonable and it makes for a good spot to work with plenty of plug sockets available should you want to settle down for a couple hours over coffee and a snack.

£
Vegan

Temple of Seitan 13

Devilishly-delicious faux chicken
419 Coldharbour Lane, SW9 8LH
www.templeofseitan.co.uk
Insta: @templeofseitan
Travel: Brixton LU
Mon-Fri 16:00-22:00, Sat-Sun 12:00-22:00

Temple of Seitan hardly needs introducing. They took the chicken shop - one of Britain's most popular street foods - and transformed it into a plant-based treat. As pioneers of vegan street food, they've enjoyed instant success, with one shop now becoming three, so that those long queues are now spread across the capital in search of deep-fried seitan. Seitan (or wheat 'meat') might sound a tad glutinous for your liking, but the Temple's faux chicken isn't far off the real deal you'd get from KFC and its ilk. The batter balances crunch against the bite of the chick'n, creating a texture that's difficult to differentiate from the original. Their other offerings, like burgers and wraps, are equally good, and of course, all those essential extras like chips, slaw and mac n' cheese are available, with burgers and wings costing around £7 and sides around £4. Now that they are popping up all over London, there's no excuse not to ditch your Dixy's and try one of the capital's most popular plant-based indulgences.

£-££
Vegan

Branches at:
43 Parkway, Camden, NW1 7PN (see p.95)
5 Morning Lane, Hackney, E9 6NA (see p.284)

VSource ⓮

Vegan Caribbean takeout
107 Dulwich Road, SE24 0NG
0742 4714 780
Insta: @vsource17
Travel: Herne Hill Rail
Mon-Fri 12:00-19:00, Sat 10:00-18:00

Tucked away in a corner of Brockwell Park, VSource is a discreet diner for getting takeout vegan Caribbean cuisine. As well as serving up some fusion takes on staple English dishes like cooked breakfast and fish & chips, they dish out all those favourites you'd expect, from callaloo patties to plantain-adorned lentil curries. They also have filling indulgences like dumplings or mac 'n cheese. It's easiest to opt for a platter, which allows you to mix and match between what's on offer amongst the various grains, mains and sides available, and which cost between £10 and £12. Be mindful that you won't be able to sit indoors, so be prepared for a take-home or a meal in the wonderful Brockwell Park, which is just opposite.

£-££
Vegan

BROCA

BROCKLEY

The Broca

Brockley's favourite café
3 & 4 Coulgate Street, SE4 2RW
020 7277 7888
www.thebroca.com
Insta: @thebrocacafe
Travel: Brockley LO
Daily 08:00-16:00

Brockley might be a part of London that is out of sight for some, but if you ever find yourself fortunate enough to wander out of the station, then Broca is hard to miss. The bright yellow façade catches the eye and inside it's a homely local café that has become something of an institution. The café has formed quite a community among the locals, and they even have their own @dogsofbroca Instagram page for the furry friends of regulars.

Broca Café has mastered the art of bringing comforting hot drinks, as well as veggie and vegan brunches to the hungery citizens of Brockley. The 'Meatless Full English', waffles, sandwiches and cakes are all available here, plus artisan coffee. They also serve alcoholic beverages too if that takes your fancy. The food and drinks are all great value and Broca has lots of outdoor seating for when the weather is fine and a shabby chic interior for when it's chilly. If you need top quality organic groceries, then Broca is also the best go-to in the area, stocking everything from dried and jarred goods to fresh bread and eggs.

£
Vegetarian

DEPTFORD & NEW CROSS

The Waiting Room

Bagels and banter at this grungy diner
142 Deptford High Street, SE8 3PQ
www.waitingroomse8.co.uk
Insta: @waitingroomse8
Travel: Deptford Rail
Mon-Wed 08:00-15:00, Thur-Fri 08:00-22:00,
Sat 09:00-22:00, Sun 09:00-16:00

This narrow little café is a friendly spot located towards the end of Deptford Market and has a loyal following, with lots of regulars showing up to chow down while they chat away. Popular dishes include their burgers and chick'n (served from midday), as well as their loaded hash browns and brunch rolls stuffed with avo cream and sausages. But their real superpower is their vegan reinventions of the Brick Lane bagel (served until 3 pm daily). And don't worry, prices aren't ramped up in comparison to their meat counterpart, for the classic 'Champ' with 'ham' slices, cheese, pickle, tomato and slathered in mustard costs just £4.70.

The small space has bags of individuality and quirkiness – assorted posters and wacky statues are all over the place and you'll find books and even VHS' to exchange. The quirkiness extends to the menu including 'Seitanic Wings' with 'Deptford Death Sauce' and 'Mammoth Maiden' brunch rolls. As well as being fun and tasty, the food is great value and the portions generous. It's a friendly place to sit and relax and they also do a great takeout service.

£
Vegan

CHEESE
PATRONS ONLY

MACKEREL
LONG LIVE THE
MARAUDING WAYS
BLUE BRICK CAFE

EAST DULWICH

The Blue Brick Café

Dulwich's most iconic café
14 Fellbrigg Road, SE22 9HH
020 8299 8670
www.cargocollective.com/bluebrickcafe
Insta: @bluebrickcafe
Travel: East Dulwich Rail
Mon-Sat 09:00-17:30, Sun 09:30-17:00

The Blue Brick Café is a charming neighbourhood café spot in the slightly sleepy heart of south London. The eponymous blue brickwork and classic typography provide the perfect façade to a homely interior that is filled with natural light and a mix of vintage furniture and homewares. It is the perfect brunch location, come rain or shine, and not just for its cosy atmosphere - they know how to do food and drink too. Everything here is vegetarian or vegan and uses fresh, seasonal produce and artisan products like Climpson & Sons coffee, belying the premises' past as a greasy spoon (although you can still order breakfast around the clock). Tasty soups, fragrant salads and spicy stews make up the bulk of their menu, but you can also get a comforting bowl of spaghetti or a meat-free fry-up if you fancy. They have other breakfast options and a host of great pastries, cakes and desserts. Quality food and drink doesn't come at a premium here, with plentiful breakfasts, brunches or lunches only costing between £5 and £10. We're thoroughly jealous of the citizens of Dulwich who get to call The Blue Brick Café their local - a 5-star London eatery.

£
Vegetarian

ELEPHANT & CASTLE, VAUXHALL & LAMBETH

1. Beza
2. Café at Jamyang
3. Café Van Gogh
4. Kinder Kitchen
5. The Ragged Canteen

A) Fareshares (see p.330)

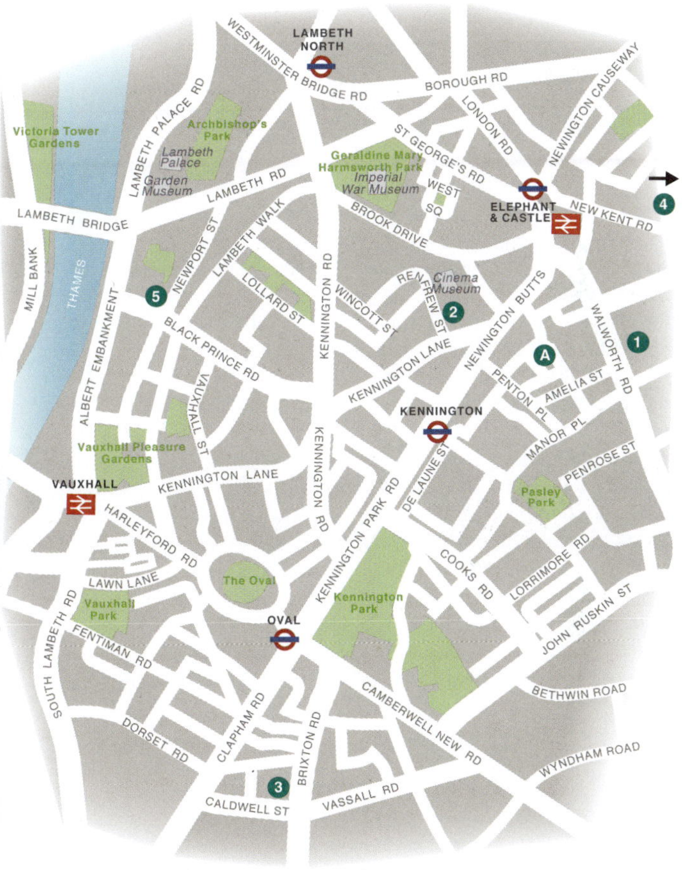
LAMBETH NORTH
WESTMINSTER BRIDGE RD
BOROUGH RD
NEWINGTON CAUSEWAY
LONDON RD
ST GEORGE'S RD
Victoria Tower Gardens
LAMBETH PALACE RD
Archbishop's Park
Lambeth Palace
Garden Museum
Geraldine Mary Harmsworth Park
Imperial War Museum
WEST SQ
LAMBETH RD
ELEPHANT & CASTLE
NEW KENT RD
4
LAMBETH BRIDGE
BROOK DRIVE
MILL BANK
THAMES
NEWPORT ST
LAMBETH WALK
LOLLARD ST
KENNINGTON RD
WINCOTT ST
RENFREW ST
Cinema Museum
2
NEWINGTON BUTTS
WALWORTH RD
1
5
ALBERT EMBANKMENT
BLACK PRINCE RD
KENNINGTON LANE
A
PENTON PL
AMELIA ST
VAUXHALL ST
KENNINGTON
MANOR PL
Vauxhall Pleasure Gardens
PENROSE ST
DE LAUNE ST
VAUXHALL
KENNINGTON LANE
KENNINGTON RD
KENNINGTON PARK RD
Pasley Park
HARLEYFORD RD
COOKS RD
LORRIMORE RD
The Oval
LAWN LANE
Vauxhall Park
Kennington Park
JOHN RUSKIN ST
OVAL
FENTIMAN RD
SOUTH LAMBETH RD
CAMBERWELL NEW RD
BETHWIN ROAD
DORSET RD
CLAPHAM RD
BRIXTON RD
WYNDHAM ROAD
3
VASSALL RD
CALDWELL ST

Beza ❶

Ethiopian vegan restaurant
8A Sayer St, Walworth, SE17 1FH
0783 346 3095
Insta: @bezaethio
Travel: Elephant & Castle LU
Tue-Sat 12:00-22:00

Beza is a family-run affair, staffed by students and friends close to the eponymous owner. The stylish restaurant is also very much part of the local community and funded cooking for NHS staff, the homeless and people struggling to make ends meet during lockdown. As for the food, you'll find a table full of colour with stews made from spinach, tomatoes and beans of every variety. This is thanks to the Orthodox Christian values that influence much of Ethiopian cuisine and make it entirely vegan. All these colourful dishes are served alongside injera, the region's most famous dish, which is a kind of sourdough flatbread that is perfect for scooping up the curries and sauces. Best for when with friends, at Beza we recommend you order a platter, so you can share and enjoy the full variety of stews on offer. Depending on the size of your party, expect to spend between £10 and £15 per person, but whatever you choose you'll eat exceptionally well and feel all the better for it with a menu that is all-natural, healthy and vegan. The space includes some traditional Ethiopian tables which are ideal for serving their strong and flavourful coffee, which is always the perfect way to end a meal here.

££
Vegan

BEZA

Courtyard Café at Jamyang ❷

The epitome of an urban oasis

43 Renfrew Road, SE11 4NA
020 7820 8787
www.jamyang.co.uk/cafe
Insta: @cafeatjamyang
Travel: Kennington LU
Fri-Sun 10:00-15:00

Nestled within the ever-tranquil grounds of the Jamyang London Buddhist Centre, at the Courtyard Café you could completely forget you're only a stone's throw from the chaotic goings on around the Elephant & Castle. And now that the café hosts the former chefs from the much-loved Bonnington Café, there's another reason to visit this peaceful place. Their ever-changing menu, which features dishes ranging from miso soups to jackfruit stews, is created from City Harvest donations of surplus vegetables, making them not only ethical and sustainable but also a healthy alternative to the sea of surrounding takeouts that lie just beyond the walls. And of course, the Buddhist practice of abstaining from harming animals is carried over, so all the food is vegetarian or vegan. With lunch usually costing between £8 and £12, and smaller dishes like cake or soup between £3 and £5, there's no need to worry about scrimping. For those who might struggle to pay, the café also provides free community meals. There are also amazing community workshops run here: from kimchi-making to drawing classes, so get down to the Courtyard Café for a spot of rest and relaxation.

£
Vegetarian

Café Van Gogh ❸

International vegan
88 Brixton Road, SW9 6BE
07546 966 554
www.cafevangogh.co.uk
Insta: @cafevangogh01
Travel: Oval LU
Mon 09:00-15:00, Tue-Wed 09:00-16:00 & 17:00-21:00,
Thur-Fri 09:00-16:00 & 17:00-22:00,
Sat 10:00-15:30 & 17:00-22:00, Sun 09:00-16:30

Plant-based eateries strive for 'guilt-free' eating, but Café Van Gogh is not just 100% vegan and waste-free but is also a non-profit organisation. They work with an employment charity, to train and employ people with disabilities and also have a 'pay it forward' scheme where anyone can buy a 'suspended coffee' (or any non-alcoholic drink) for someone to claim at a later point.

Beyond their social good, this café has a warmth and charm to it. Sitting adjacent to a church in a small, listed brick-clad building, the interior is punctuated with lush houseplants and a spiral staircase at its centre that leads up to a beautiful mural depicting a starry night sky inspired by Van Gogh. If you prefer to eat alfresco they have an equally leafy patio to enjoy in the summer months. Their seasonal menu changes regularly but expect to find hearty favourites like burgers, bangers & mash, dhal and jerk plantain. The portions are generous and everything is reasonably priced. It's little wonder why this is such a local favourite with great food and the community at the heart of what they do.

£-££
Vegan

Kinder Kitchen ❹

Not just for kids!

27 Bartholomew St, London SE1 4AL
020 3971 2450
www.kinderkitchen.london
Insta: @kinderkitchense1
Travel: Elephant & Castle LU
Mon-Fri 09:00-15:00, Sat-Sun 09:00-16:00

Kinder Kitchen is a plant-based café that runs in partnership with kindergartens, providing them with nutritious vegan food. On this sleepy side street, just a stone's throw from Elephant & Castle, the grown-ups are catered for. The menu is an exercise in 'less, but better', with only those classic breakfast and brunch dishes that we all know and love, like porridge with maple syrup, crumbled nuts, cinnamon and fresh fruit, or the Full English, cheese toasties, brownies and croissants - all of which are delicious and freshly prepared.

With baked goods for as little as £2.50, and breakfasts between £3.50 and £5.50 (save for the Full English at £9), you'll also fail to find anywhere better value in London, vegan or otherwise. The aesthetics of the interior demonstrates the owners' eye for good design as well - the space was an abandoned hair salon before its transformation into a pastel-coloured celebration of 1970s café style. Kinder Kitchen is the kind of place you'll wish was on your doorstep, so whether nearby or not, don't hesitate to try it.

£
Vegan

The Ragged Canteen 5

Locally-sourced lunches

Beaconsfield Gallery, 22 Newport Street, SE11 6AY
020 7582 6465
www.beaconsfield.ltd.uk/café
Insta: @raggedcanteen
Travel: Vauxhall LU
Tue-Sun 11:00-17:00, lunch served between 12:00-14:00

Located in the Beaconsfield Gallery, this artfully minimal space offers vegetarian and vegan brunches, lunches and amazing homemade baked goods that call for a visit in their own right. The passion they have for sourcing their food ethically shows in their daily changing seasonal menu, which also has plenty of gluten-free options.

The Ragged Canteen makes an effort to source food from local urban growers and foragers. The produce is used to create colourful dishes that take their inspiration from around the world, as can be seen on the canteen's Instagram feed. You can expect to find salads, sandwiches and specials that taste as good as they look. Despite all this effort, the prices are very reasonable and the canteen has a loyal following among local office workers. Expect to spend around £6 to £7 for a good brunch or lunch, and less for an exceptionally tasty coffee and cake. The Ragged Canteen is part of the Beaconsfield Gallery and eating here is a great opportunity to catch up on the gallery's changing programme of events and exhibitions. With free WiFi and a terrace for the summer, the only thing this eatery lacks is meat, so for veggies, vegans and the curious alike, be sure to schedule a visit.

£
Vegetarian

PECKHAM

1. Deserted Cactus / Rons Coffee House
2. En Root Peckham
3. naïfs
4. Omni
5. Persepolis
6. Zionly Manna

PECKHAM HIGH ST
RYE LANE
HANOVER PARK
CLAYTON RD
CONSORT RD
Cossall Park
CERISE RD
CICELY RD
BELLENDEN RD
HIGHSHORE RD
ELM GROVE
PECKHAM RYE
HOLLY GROVE
Bussey Building
BLENHEIM GROVE
BOURNEMOUTH RD
CHOUMERT RD
CHADWICK RD
COPELAND RD
BRAYARDS RD
CONSORT RD
Consort Park
CHOUMERT GROVE
ALPHA ST
HEATON RD
MCDERMOTT RD
ANSTEY ST
NIGEL RD
MAXTED RD
WINGFIELD ST
HOWDEN ST
NUTBROOK ST
PECKHAM RYE
SCYLLA RD
PECKHAM RYE
PECKHAM RYE PARK
1
2
3
4
5
6

Deserted Cactus ❶

Hearty vegan caribbean food
Holdron's Arcade, Unit 23 & 25,
135A Peckham Rye, SE15 4ST
Insta: @deserted_cactus
Travel: Peckham Rye LO
Thur & Sat 13:00-16:00

You'll be hard-pressed to find a hole-in-the wall serving vegan grub as good as Deserted Cactus. Bowls full of the best of Afro-Caribbean cooking such as butterbean curries and pumpkin stews. Esme is the owner/cook and she operates very limited opening hours and offers no menu. This way of doing things seems to work as she has a loyal following and plenty of visitors drawn by her popular YouTube channel with videos covering everything from recipes to shopping hauls. If you're in Peckham and visiting Holdron's Arcade outside Esme's very narrow opening times you might like to try Rons - see opposite.

£
Vegan

Branch

En Root Peckham ❷

Old-school fare for a brand-new crowd
28 Peckham Rye, SE15 4JR
www.enrootldn.co.uk
Full review see p.190

Rons Coffee House ❶

A peerless Peckham café
Holdrons Arcade,135a Rye Lane, SE15 4ST
www.ronspeckham.com
Insta: @ronspeckham
Travel: Peckham Rye LO
Wed-Thur 08:00-18:00, Fri 08:00-21:00,
Sat 09:00-21:00, Sun 09:00-16:00

Nestled within Holdrons Arcade, next to the iconic Khan's Bargain store, it's difficult to miss Rons Coffee House. Signature dishes that reward visitors include the best vegan beans on toast in Britain - served using rosemary focaccia with their tahini rarebit, this is as gourmet as that hallowed dish can get. Or else, try the teriyaki tofu bok choi ciabatta, which is as delicious as it is onomatopoeic, aided in part by the filling of smacked cucumber, Asian salsa and sriracha mayo. Or else the oyster mushroom bacon muffin which, with its punchy chive mayo and chilli & tomato relish, is a yummy vegan breakfast. With sandwiches starting for as little as £4.70, you have no excuse not to try them for yourself, plus there's great coffee and pastries for when you need that little extra something. Soups change daily, but it's the cookies we can't get enough of. With plenty of natural light, abundant house plants and modern wooden furnishings - the place is a friendly oasis and even your dog is welcome. Check out their social media for evening events to come in the near future.

£
Vegan

naïfs ❸

The best vegan bistro
56 Goldsmith Road, SE15 5TN
020 3490 2422
www.naifs.co.uk
Insta: @naifsrestaurant
Travel: Queen's Road Peckham LO
Thur-Sat 18:00-23:00

naïfs is exactly what London's vegan restaurant scene has been needing. Food that looks as good as it tastes, served in a beautifully simple interior fitted with modern, comfortable furniture. Combined with natural wine and swanky cocktails, this makes for the kind of bijou night out plant-based punters have been denied for all too long. Their focus is on local and organic produce, served up sharing style on small plates to spread the love around - akin to mezze - with appetisers and desserts to be added on as extras. The set menu takes the stress away, so you can lean back and focus on the food, which is amongst the best meat-free fare to be found. Fried king oysters, lentil pâté, yam fritters or rhubarb and vanilla ice cream, are just some of the things to take your fancy. £27 gets you six courses, and their other plates cost £10 or less, so you can eat like a royal without extortionate prices. But when it comes to the crown of vegan restaurants, naïfs may just have the most convincing of claims.

££-£££
Vegan

Omni ❹

Amazing in all ways
24a Peckham Rye, SE15 4JR
020 7450 6347
www.theomnicollective.com
Insta: @theomnicollective
Travel: Peckham Rye LO
Wed-Sat 11:30-22:30

As their name denotes, Omni are all we've been looking for in a restaurant: a chic interior within which to enjoy local, seasonal produce cooked up so well it makes you forget all about any raging debates over the ethics of food. You can choose between a £40 tasting menu which ticks all the boxes or their à la carte, which ranges between £6-£10 for dishes, for when a little less peckish, but in truth, this is one to go all out for. The menu takes you on a tour from fried artichoke heart burgers to celeriac latkas and pink lady tarte tatin, all to be exceptionally well paired with some of the most enjoyable natural wines doing the restaurant rounds. You might have to fight for a table as they're one of the more in-demand spots in Peckham. Should you get your hands on one, you'll join the many other diners that leave floating on a cloud, for this is one of the best vegan meals out in London.

££-£££
Vegan

Persepolis ❺

Middle Eastern café and deli
28-30 Peckham High Street, SE15 5DT
020 7639 8007
www.foratasteofpersia.co.uk
Insta: @persepolis_peckham
Travel: Peckham Rye Station
Daily 11.00-22.30

Hidden behind the brightly coloured façade is an establishment that encapsulates Peckham's diversity. A Persian grocery store cum-diner, it is a strange mix of beautifully woven rugs alongside kitschy knick-knacks and grocery goods. As quaint as it is queer, the décor is however still secondary to the food.

Mezzes make up the menu here, but the options are surprisingly varied and can include falafels, tabbouleh and houmous, all expertly enlivened with the addition of pomegranates, juniper and tahini. They can be relied on for their signature dishes like baked sweet potato filled with Persian baked beans and halloumi, and ever-popular vegan knickerbocker glory, alongside more traditional Persian dishes like faloodeh (sorbet). But as they state, most of their menu is 'off piste' so on any given day you can expect to try something different. The portions are generous and despite the food's light and fresh nature, you can expect to enjoy a substantial meal for around £10. With vegan and gluten-free options, this is a place worth pencilling in for a special visit. Be sure to check out the proprietor Sally Butcher's great cookbooks and store goods, which are a must-have for anybody hoping to recreate the magic here at home. Sally is usually on hand preparing the food, so if you're lucky you might be able to get a signed copy.

£
Vegetarian

Zionly Manna ❻

Caribbean vegan in Rye Lane Market

Unit 41, Rye Lane Indoor Market, SE15 5BY
0783 113 6705
Insta: @zionlymanna
Travel: Peckham Rye LO and Rail
Mon-Sat 10:00-18:00

Nestled inside Rye Lane indoor market, you'll find a restaurant that captures the soul of Peckham. Zionly Manna is a vegan eatery that serves Caribbean dishes made in-house by the Rastafarian chef and owner Jahson Peat. He cooks daily changing specials of curries, stews and vegetable salads, as well as staples like dumplings and meat-free mutton curry. You can also get some more on-trend options like falafel, liquid food juices and raw kale salads. Root beers, teas and tonics, as well as a range of cakes and other desserts, are available for just a couple of quid. Here, the plates are plentiful, and you can choose between a single dish like butter bean stew for £7 or a platter for £15 which buys you a mountain of comforting vegan grub (four dishes and three dumplings) with a canned drink, or try a bit of everything for £20 (which comes with fresh juice). The space is a little ramshackle, with only a few random chairs and tables dotted around the small hole-in-the-wall shop, but the food makes up for the decor. Zionly Manna offers top quality and authentic vegan Caribbean cuisine that beats the chain restaurants serving a poor imitation of these dishes. If you're in Peckham, this is definitely one to seek out.

£
Vegan

SOUTHWARK

Mallow

Mildred's gets a makeover in Borough Market
1 Cathedral St, SE1 9DE
020 7846 8785
www.mallowlondon.com
Insta: @mallowlondon
Travel: London Bridge LU
Daily 09:00-23:00

Mallow is the brainchild of the pioneering vegetarian restaurateurs behind Mildreds, transplanted to the foodie mecca of Borough Market. This new venture offers a market-to-table concept that uses the produce available just metres away with modern bistro cooking to offer an eclectic all-day menu that minimises waste and maximises flavour. From cauliflower chaat and porcini truffle croquettes, to shiitake dashi udon with sesame tempeh and banana blossom tacos with pistachio mole, there is so much to sink your teeth into. The plum plant burger and crème brûlée served two ways - either as a brioche French toast brunch dish, accompanied with blackberry compote and vanilla cream, or as the classic dessert - are crying out to be tried. The space is more formal than Mildreds, with swank modern wooden furnishing and orb lighting, creating an atmosphere of laid-back luxury, but prices remain reasonable with small plates for around £8 and £16 for larger ones. You can feel good about any indulgence here because Mallow gives a share of profits into Streetsmart, a charity for the homeless that they've raised over £100k for in the last 20 years. Mallow also participates in a surplus food collection service that distributes unused food within the local area.

£££
Vegan

APT
mallow
plant - based

STREATHAM

Wholemeal Café

Serving reliable veggie grub since 1978

1 Shrubbery Road, SW16 2AS
020 8769 2423
www.wholemealcafe.com
Travel: Streatham Rail
Tue-Sat 12:00-21:00

Wholemeal café is one of London's longest-running vegetarian restaurants. The fact it stood this test of time, where so many others haven't, is a testament to how the business is run. It's healthy, seasonal and local, but presented without fuss - think homemade rather than haute cuisine. Salads, stews and soups take pride of place, such as their Moroccan chickpea and tomato, or else their roast cauliflower with cumin, coriander, turmeric, paprika, garlic and soy sauce. Dessert is where the real showstopper is - banoffee pie that is well worth a detour. Drinks include organic wines and freshly squeezed juices. Starters and desserts hover around £6 and mains around twice that much. The decor and their website might seem a little dated compared to newer arrivals on the scene, but Wholemeal Café has lasted this long by concentrating on serving hearty, generous vegetarian and vegan food to the local community and long may it continue.

£-££
Vegetarian

WIMBLEDON

Amrutha Lounge

Asian-fusion vegan soul food
326 Garratt Lane, SW18 4EJ
020 8001 4628
www.amrutha.co.uk
Insta: @amruthauk
Travel: Earlsfield Rail
Tue-Thur 18:00-22:00, Fri 13:00-15:00 & 18:00-22:00,
Sat 13:00-22:00, Sun 13:00-21:00

This Asian-fusion soul food shop in South Wandsworth has been offering an eclectic mix of Indian, south-east Asian and Middle-Eastern food for a few years now and has acquired quite a following. Whilst the selection platter allows you to have a little bit of everything, you can also order plates individually, including beet gazpacho, falafels, dahl or Thai green curry. Desserts change regularly but feature dishes like Filipino plantain fritters and banoffee cheesecake. The portions here are some of the most generous to be found in the capital but are still well presented. Starters cost £6, whilst bowls and boxes are £18, but Amrutha also has a pay-what-you-like policy, so there is no risk of leaving disappointed. In terms of drinks, it's BYOB which reflects the relaxed, friendly atmosphere of the place. The interior is pared back, but comfortable and with plenty of seating, this is a great place to visit if you're in the area.

£-££
Vegan

Flat Earth Pizzas, see p.245

EAST

BETHNAL GREEN & MILE END

1. E3 Vegan
2. Flat Earth Pizzas
3. The Gallery Café
4. Jungle Electric
5. Love Shack
6. Sazzy & Fran Café
7. Young Vegans Pizza Shop

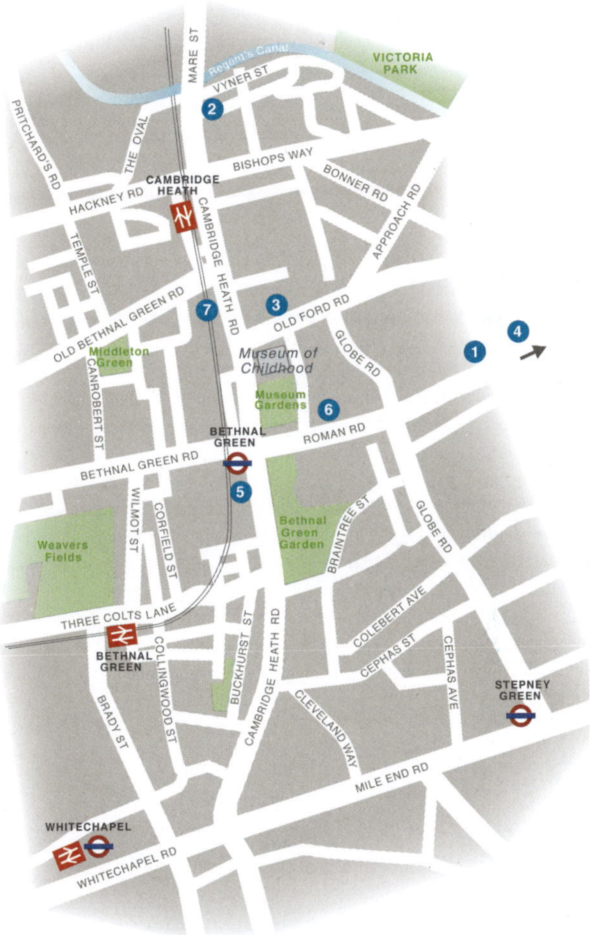

Regent's Canal
VICTORIA PARK
MARE ST
VYNER ST
PRITCHARD'S RD
THE OVAL
BISHOPS WAY
BONNER RD
CAMBRIDGE HEATH
HACKNEY RD
APPROACH RD
TEMPLE ST
CAMBRIDGE HEATH RD
OLD BETHNAL GREEN RD
OLD FORD RD
GLOBE RD
Middleton Green
CANROBERT ST
Museum of Childhood
Museum Gardens
BETHNAL GREEN
ROMAN RD
BETHNAL GREEN RD
WILMOT ST
CORFIELD ST
Weavers Fields
Bethnal Green Garden
BRAINTREE ST
GLOBE RD
THREE COLTS LANE
BETHNAL GREEN
COLLINGWOOD ST
BUCKHURST ST
CAMBRIDGE HEATH RD
COLEBERT AVE
CEPHAS ST
CEPHAS AVE
CLEVELAND WAY
STEPNEY GREEN
BRADY ST
MILE END RD
WHITECHAPEL
WHITECHAPEL RD

E3 Vegan ❶

Vegan dining from the chef behind Vanilla Black

357 Roman Road, E3 5QR
020 3859 9798
www.e3vegan.com
Insta: @e3.vegan
Travel: Mile End LU
Wed-Sun 12:00-17:00

If you've ever heard of Vanilla Black, you'll know you're in safe hands when eating at E3 Vegan, because Marc Joseph from London's first truly fine-dining vegan eatery (now closed) has found a new home in East London. It is from here that he runs a café by day while also hosting a fabulous supper club on occasional evenings. The regular menu features many things you'd expect - vegan variations of a Full English breakfast and burgers, as well as falafels, soups and salads, or otherwise a variety of cakes and coffee. You can also bag yourself a Sunday Roast or a seven-course experience on Friday evenings, but for us, the crispy celeriac schnitzel and sticky toffee pudding are the real showstoppers. Main courses will set you back about £14, with lighter dishes for £9, and sweet stuff for around half of that, so whether you're just passing by and in need of a bite to eat or in search of a somewhat more sit-down affair, E3 Vegan has you covered. We're sure once you've tried the food at the café you'll be putting your name down for one of the supper clubs where Marc can really give his culinary skills full expression.

££
Vegan

Flat Earth Pizzas ❷

No conspiracy behind these award-winning crusts

288 Cambridge Heath Road, E2 9DA
020 7998 6556
www.flatearthpizzas.com
Insta: @flatearthpizzas
Travel: Bethnal Green LU
Tue-Fri 08:00-22:00, Sat 12:00-22:00, Sun 12:00-20:00

Many things stand out about Flat Earth's pizzas, but first and foremost is how good they are. It speaks volumes that they don't just reject meat toppings but also many other standard practices within the industry that are horrible from a sustainability standpoint. For example, rather than importing Italian flour, they instead opt to use local and seasonal ingredients including heritage grains. They've also essentially cracked being a zero-waste operation, something other places drowning in a sea of cardboard and cling film could learn from. Among their vibrant flavours is their signature pizza, the 'Hackney Hot' with its pickled beetroot and jalapeño topping, which spices things up, as does their tangy 'Kimchi Fiorentina' and more classic vegan mozzarella and wild garlic variant. What's more, you can get serious brownies, natural wines and classy cocktails to go with it all. If you need something lighter during the daytime then they offer brunch dishes too. Pizzas are priced between £10 and £15, which is in keeping with other pizzerias in the area, so do yourself and the planet a favour, and get down to Flat Earth Pizza.

££
Vegetarian

The Gallery Café ❸

Hackney's hub for everything vegan

Margaret's House Settlement,
21 Old Ford Road, E2 9PL
020 8980 2092
www.stmargaretshouse.org.uk
Insta: @st.margarets.house
Daily 08:30-18:00

Unlike many London eateries that try and often fail to keep up with fads and fashions, the Gallery Café is an old-school vegan eatery. It can double as either your local or as part of a vegan-friendly day trip, being situated a short stroll from Bethnal Green station and neighbouring the Young V&A.

The food here is ethically sourced, wholesome and unpretentious. Breakfast runs from 9am till noon, and the main menu from then until 4pm, 7 days a week. They also have a rotation of seasonal specials, fresh sandwiches and sweet treats, meaning you're unlikely to run out of things to try. Meals cost £6-£9, drinks between £2 and £4, and their hearty Full English is definitely one to try. The Gallery Café is part of a community-based charity, St. Margaret's House - so look out for their yoga classes, charity clothing boutique and cultural events throughout the year.

£
Vegan

Jungle Electric 4

Roman Road's new vegan neighbour

467 Roman Road, E3 5LX
020 8616 1919
www.jungleelectric.co.uk
Insta: @jungle.electric
Travel: Bow Road LU
Mon-Fri 09:00-17:00, Sat 09:00-18:00, Sun 10:00-16:00

This self-described indie coffee shop is a fantastic neighbourhood café for anyone within a stone's throw of Victoria Park, whether for their exceptionally reasonable coffee and cake for a fiver deal, or anyone looking to find a good place to work whilst tucking into a toastie. The classic toasted sandwich is the menu's signature dish, coming as it does with a wide variety of familiar fillings, from cheese that isn't cheese to 'tunah' or faux sausage. At around £6, it's certainly one of the most affordable lunches to be found in the area. Their chocolate brownies and hot cocoas will leave you wondering how on earth they weren't made with dairy, as the convincing creaminess is almost criminally suspect! Otherwise, their menu rotates regularly, as does the roster of local musicians, stand-up comedians and slam poets they host for live events, which are open to applications if you happen to be an aspiring talent too. Last but not least, this is a very dog-friendly establishment, so if you happen to have finished up a walk in East London's premier park for pooches nearby, then get on down here.

£
Vegan

Love Shack Vegan ❺

Hackney's hippie hangout

Arch 298, 299 Cambridge Heath Road, E2 9HA
0771 775 6709
www.loveshackldn.com
Insta: @loveshack_ldn
Travel: Bethnal Green LU
Mon-Tue 18:00-23:00, Wed-Thur 18:00-00:00, Fri 18:00-01:30, Sat 11:00-01:30, Sun 11:00-23:00

Cambridge Heath meets Koh Phi Phi at this plastic-free patch of land, which aims to turn an industrial stretch of street into a typical Thai island hangout. Love Shack comes equipped with everything you would've once least expected to find under an East London railway arch (although how times have changed): hammocks, sun loungers and bean bags laid out across their stretch of semi alfresco turf, and an offering of global vegan grub during the day before yoga sessions, comedy nights and pottery classes. However, it is more in line with expectations if you've ever visited a backpacker café, where granola bowls, faux meat burgers and anything involving houmous make up the staples of the menu, for around £15 per main dish and half as much for smaller plates. On top of that, mushroom shakes (not the trippy kind) have their very own section. With these, you get to choose from a wealth of ingredients, spanning lion's mane to cordyceps. The interior has a bohemian aesthetic, and Love Shack is a great choice for those with a four-legged friend - bring the pooch along for 10% off your bill.

££
Vegan

Sazzy & Fran Café 6

Sandwiches to make you a superfan

33 Roman Road, E2 0HU
07428 717 579
www.sazzyandfrancafe.com
Insta: @sazzyandfrancafe
Travel: Cambridge Heath LO/Bethnal Green LU
Mon-Fri 07:30-17:00, Sat & Sun 09:00-17:00

Beginning its life in a shipping container, Sazzy & Fran have now founded a café on Roman road. Run by the eponymous couple, they serve all the café classics: 'cheese' toasties, BLTs, bagels, soups and pancakes, as well as more low-key vegan cravings like their elevated version of peanut butter on toast. Another favourite is their 'zalmon' and cream cheese bagel which uses slivers of carrot in a citrus marinade and is unbelievably convincing. The cooking is simple and wholesome but what really shines through all their dishes is the high quality of produce and the attention to detail.

They have an ever-changing range of baked goods, from croissants to gooey brownies and muffins – there is something for both the sweet and savoury toothed here, with delicious Climpson & Sons coffee to match. The interior is as homely as the food, and they even have a resident dog to cuddle up to or to introduce to your own four-legged friend. Sazzy & Fran Café is a good choice when looking for a quality quick bite in this corner of Hackney, and they also offer a takeaway service for when just passing through.

££
Vegan

Young Vegans Pizza Shop 7

A slice of Brooklyn in Bethnal Green
393 Cambridge Heath Rd, E2 9RA
020 8923 0297
www.youngveganspizzashop.com
Insta: @youngveganspizzashop
Travel: Bethnal Green LU
Wed-Sat 17:00-22:00

You know you're in luck when you can have lasagne as a side. Young Vegans Pizza Shop is indulging everyone's dairy desires, without any of the hangups, with plant-based cheeses on their pies and pasta that are as convincing as can be, thanks to the fact their vegan mozzarella is made in-house. The cheese is such a perfect product that over one hundred other pizzerias in the UK source it from here. You can stick to the classics like Margherita or familiar favourites like 'the Truffled' if you want, but a lot more fun can be had with things like 'the Filthy Weekend', which features the most sacrilegious of toppings - ham & pineapple - or their 'Cheezeburger', a combo that shouldn't but just does work. The mozzarella sticks, cannelloni and parm are some more Italian-American inventions we can't get enough of. Pizzas go for £13, whilst sides range between £4 and £8, so you can eat well without worrying about the bill, but you might need to unbutton somewhat by the end of the night. There's plenty of indoor seating for nights out with friends, and be sure to mentally bookmark the shop for whenever those takeout nights strike.

££
Vegan

YOUNG
VEGANS

DALSTON

1. Andu Café
2. Essential Vegan Kitchen / Dalston Superstore
3. Helma
4. Mildred's Dalston
5. Oowee Vegan
6. Plates

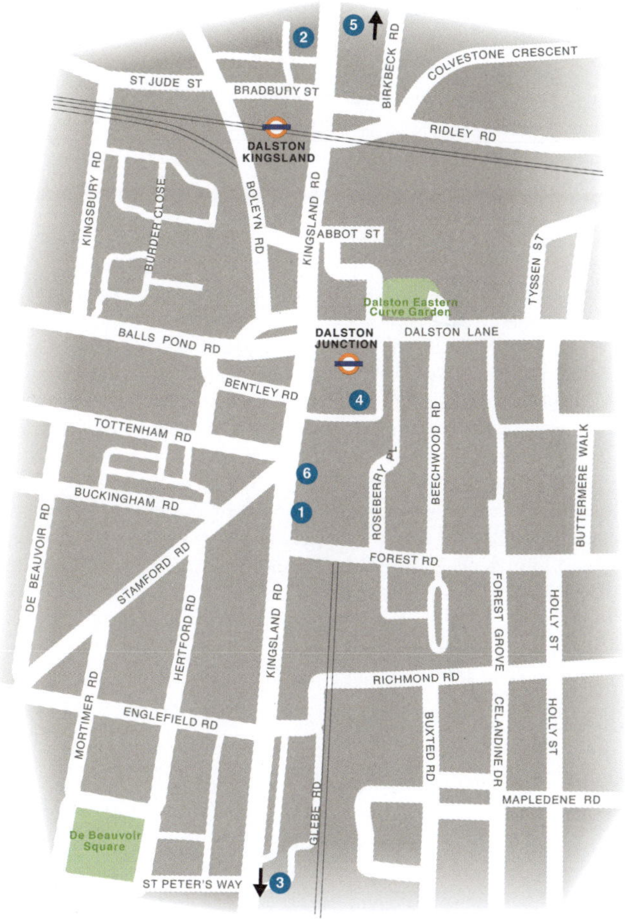
2
5
ST JUDE ST
BRADBURY ST
BIRKBECK RD
COLVESTONE CRESCENT
RIDLEY RD
DALSTON KINGSLAND
KINGSBURY RD
BURDER CLOSE
BOLEYN RD
KINGSLAND RD
ABBOT ST
TYSSEN ST
Dalston Eastern Curve Garden
BALLS POND RD
DALSTON JUNCTION
DALSTON LANE
BENTLEY RD
4
TOTTENHAM RD
ROSEBERRY PL
BEECHWOOD RD
BUTTERMERE WALK
6
BUCKINGHAM RD
1
DE BEAUVOIR RD
STAMFORD RD
HERTFORD RD
FOREST RD
FOREST GROVE
HOLLY ST
RICHMOND RD
MORTIMER RD
ENGLEFIELD RD
BUXTED RD
CELANDINE DR
MAPLEDENE RD
GLEBE RD
De Beauvoir Square
ST PETER'S WAY
3

Andu Café 1

Homely Ethiopian café
528 Kingsland Road, E8 4AH
020 7254 1780
www.anduvegancafe.com
Travel: Dalston Junction LO
Daily 12:00-22:00

This eatery is a world away from the trend-following vegan spots you would typically associate with Hackney. The sourdough you'll find here won't come with avocado, but instead as a traditional 'injera' – a spongy flatbread that is perfect for soaking up the rich stews that are typical of Ethiopian cuisine. In fact, Ethiopia is a vegan heartland and is the inspiration behind Rastafarianism's vegan diet. Andu Café is a good first stop for getting a taste of this healthy cuisine that uses lots of legumes and spinach and enlivens these ingredients with the judicious use of spices. The food comes out as a platter for you to mix and match, which is a great way to sample a range of dishes. The café is a bit of a mishmash itself, with wood cladding and brick effect wallpaper, but the result is homely and the staff friendly, always on hand to give advice if needed. Andu Café is a pleasant place for a casual lunch or dinner and you're unlikely to pay more than £10 for a comprehensive meal, or if you opt for takeout, as little as £6. They are rightly proud of their Ethiopian coffee too, which is traditionally prepared and is a perfect end to a meal here.

£
Vegan

Essential Vegan Kitchen ❷

London's first and only vegan Brazilian café
117 Kingsland High Street, E8 2PB
020 7254 2273
www.essentialvegan.uk
Insta: @essentialvegan
Travel: Dalston Kingsland LO
Tue-Fri 16:00-21:00, Sat 12:00-21:00, Sun 12:00-19:00

Some readers may well remember in the days before the pandemic that Essential Vegan Kitchen started life as a café adjacent to Arnold Circus in Shoreditch. Since then, it has found a new home in one of London's best-known nightlife venues - Dalston Superstore. This makes a lot of sense once you consider how much the Brazilian spirit of dance lives through this vibrant vegan cooking. Dishes are as diverse as 'salgadinhos' - deep-fried potato cheese balls, plantain stews, their 'Full Brazilian' - which puts a spin on this classic with the addition of smoked black beans and avocado, toasties, burgers and of course the artisan vegan cheeses they produce in-house. Prices for mains are nearly all under £10 and sides for around half of that, making Essential one of the more affordable spots in the area. Nestled inside this most colourful of clubs, the interior is more like a bar than a restaurant, but the leather booths make this a comfy place to relax and enjoy some quality vegan chow.

£-££
Vegan

Helma 3

Multicultural community café
13c Downham Rd, N1 5AA
www.helmalondon.com
Insta: @helmalondon
Travel: Haggerston LO
Mon-Thur 08:00-16:00, Fri & Sat 08:00-20:00, Sun 21:00-15:00

This café is run by a couple who are veterans in the restaurant business and combine this with their native knowledge of Georgian wine and Swedish fermentation to offer some of the best vegetarian food and drink to be found in the city. Their all-day breakfast is unmissable, featuring a buckwheat crêpe, which comes with comice pear, sweet dukkah, maple syrup and cashew cream. Their regularly rotating roster of cereals, soups and sandwiches are all delicious and made in-house, with local (where possible) and seasonal produce. The wine list takes a tour of the very best of Old-World natural producers - with Georgian wines taking pride of place. Dishes range in price between £6 and £12. Tess and Kosta operated the space as a socially-distanced hub for the local community during the pandemic and now have a loyal following, but you too can join the lunchtime crowd at this commendable café. They also have a Camden branch (see p.80).

££
Vegetarian

Branch

Mildred's Dalston 4

International
1 Dalston Square, E8 3GU
020 8017 1815
Full review see p.56

Helma

Oowee Dalston 5

Food so good it makes you say...

50 Stoke Newington Road, N16 7XB
020 7254 2777
www.ooweevegan.com
Insta: @oowee_vegan
Travel: Dalston Kingsland LO
Daily 11:30-23:00

This one is for the cheat days, and the indulgence of all those meaty desires you may have been avoiding. Think big ol' beef burgers, stacked chick'n burgers, even more fried chick'n, sides like dirty fries loaded with cheese and jalapenos, or other bits and bobs like tater tots, mac n cheese, onion rings plus shakes or beer depending on your stripe. These are meat substitutes at their best, which is why it's little wonder people have been ooweeing up and down the country – they've now got 2 branches in both London and Bristol, plus another in Brighton. And you can hardly blame them - burgers only cost between £5 and £10, sides and drinks for around half as much as that, meaning you can expect to eat well for around the same cost as almost any of the other high-street fast-food chains, without the ethical hangup. Unlike a lot of its vegan fast food competitors, Oowee offers plenty of seating to relax, providing a brief respite from the hustle and bustle of Dalston.

£-££
Vegan

Plates 6

Stay late at Plates

538 Kingsland Road, E8 4AH
020 7096 1307
www.plates-london.com
Insta: @plates_london
Travel: Dalston Junction LO
Wed-Thur 18:00-00:00, Fri-Sat 17:00-01:00

Although Plates has now been joined by a handful of other fine-dining vegan establishments, these guys were pioneers when they started in 2017, and remain so today. The brother-sister duo that founded it has experience from some of the most respected kitchens in the world, including the 3-starred French Laundry. Their current residency at the Untitled bar in Dalston now means you can drop by for bar snacks and cocktails, or otherwise book a table for their illustrious set menu. It's a tour de force that highlights the highest possibilities of cooking with vegetables, whilst including treats like croquettes, celeriac lasagna, and tiramisu ice cream sandwiches. At £46 per person, it's on the more expensive side of nights out for vegans, but everything on the bar menu is under £10 should you not fancy the full five courses. The setting is as Brutalist as can be - all concrete and marble, with contemporary art aplenty - making it as photogenic as the food. Plates is also one of the few vegan restaurants that stays open until the early hours, making them perfect if looking to extend the night at one of Dalston's many nearby nightclubs.

£££
Vegan

HACKNEY SOUTH

1. Aya & Suki
2. Black Cat Café
3. EDIT
4. Facing Heaven
5. The Grand Howl
6. The Spread Eagle
7. Sutton & Son's Vegan Chip Shop
8. Temple of Hackney
9. WAVE (We Are Vegan Everything)

Shops:

A) Grains & Green, see p.333

DOWNS PARK RD
PEMBURY RD
CLARENCE RD
LOWER CLAPTON RD
BLURTON RD
DUNLACE RD
MEDIAN RD
CLIFDEN RD
CHATSWORTH RD
Clapton Square
2
LWR CLAPTON RD
URSWICK RD
HOMERTON GROVE
HACKNEY DOWNS
DALSTON LN
AMHURST RD
MARE ST
9
HOMERTON HIGH ST
BARNABUS RD
6
HACKNEY CENTRAL
HOMERTON
MORNING LANE
8
GRAHAM RD
7
CHATHAM PL
WICK RD
5
KENTON RD
DARNLEY RD
A
RICHMOND RD
WELL ST
LODDIGES RD
CASSLAND RD
GASCOYNE RD
London Fields
LONDON FIELDS
3
Well Street Common
LAMB LN
WELL ST
STORE RD
AINSWORTH RD
LAURISTON RD
VICTORIA PARK RD
4
BROADWAY MRKT
WESTGATE ST
B
1
SHEEP LANE
VICTORIA PARK RD
Regent's Canal
VICTORIA PARK
GROVE RD

Aya & Suki ❶

First-class cooking from the fertile crescent

62 Broadway Market, E8 4QJ
020 7687 0236
www.ayaandsuki.com
Insta: @ayaandsuki
Travel: London Fields LO
Mon-Thur 10:00-16:00, Fri & Sat 10:00-22:30, Sun 10:00-17:00

Aya & Suki go above and beyond traditional Levantine cuisine. Think of dates, figs, olive oil, pistachios, harissa, houmous, yoghurt or pomegranate, all of which are put to use in making mezze dishes, from the light and refreshing like moutabal (aubergine dip) or fattoush (a vibrant salad), to the indulgent - stuffed filo pastries or fritters. Also, there are few better ways to start the day than with a hearty serving of shakshuka - eggs baked in a rich tomato and pepper sauce, or else their scrambled eggs with za'atar, both of which can be enjoyed alongside their weekend brunch offering, and are bound to relieve any hangover, or make the perfect preamble to a Sunday afternoon exploring the area. As if this wasn't enough, Levantine cuisine is food of the people, meaning that mezze is inexpensive - expect to pay between £5 to £8 per portion (or a tad more for bigger dishes), ideally to be shared with friends. Aya & Suki's interior mirrors the homely hospitality the region is famous for, so they're great for a dinner date, but also as a takeaway spot during Broadway Market's busy weekends. And if you've been wondering when the v-word would come up, it hasn't needed to - Levantine food is naturally oriented toward being vegetarian or vegan owing to its origins, so you can forget fake meats and enjoy this culinary adventure.

£-££
Vegetarian

Black Cat Café ❷

Workers' co-op café
76A Clarence Road, E5 8HB
020 8985 7091
www.blackcatcafe.co.uk
Insta: @blackcathackney
Travel: Hackney Central LO
Mon, Thur-Fri 11:30-16:00, Sat-Sun 10:00-16:00

Black Cat Café is a great casual vegan eatery; inexpensive, tasty and with extremely generous portions, it makes for a sound alternative to your local greasy spoon in Hackney. Tofish and chips, vegan fry-ups and seitan burgers are the kinds of hearty food you'll find here, served up by friendly volunteers in a casual and comfortable interior.

They've got lighter salad options, hot drinks and highly popular milkshakes too. You can easily eat here for around a tenner, or you can opt for their £5 soup of the day served with fresh bread and the drinks are also great value. As ethical and cooperative establishments go, Black Cat Café ticks all the boxes. After one visit it's easy to see why this place is among many vegans' favourite eateries and one well worth seeking out in the backstreets of Hackney.

£
Vegan

EDIT ③

Hackney goes 'hyper seasonal'
217 Mare Street, E8 3QE
www.edit.london
Insta: @edit.restaurant
Travel: Hackney Central LO
Mon-Tue 12:00-16:00, Wed-Fri 12:00-16:00, 17:00-23:00,
Sat-Sun 12:00-23:00

EDIT is the most recent outgrowth of Hackney's vegan dining landscape, an apt word considering their focus on sustainable and seasonable plant-based dishes, using only ingredients sourced from small-scale farms, foragers, and independent producers, whilst striving to be zero-waste. The daily changing menu features things like roasted salsify and crispy brussels sprouts, or else wild mushroom fricassee and seaweed cured celeriac atop purple potato mash. These can be enjoyed either à la carte or as part of a six-course tasting menu, with each course paired with natural wines and ciders. Their cheeseboard shows off the local talent of artisan vegan cheese makers, whilst dessert takes us back to basics with the likes of bread-and-butter pudding, only elevated by the addition of hibiscus poached pears. EDIT's founder has used their architectural training to create an ever-so-attractive space, where the brick walls and iron columns from the former factory building in which the restaurant resides, contrast with the recycled and reclaimed wooden furnishings. While their bar and courtyard area are kept for walk-ins, it's best to reserve a table to avoid disappointment.

£££
Vegan

Facing Heaven ❹

Dan-dan noodles that channel the divine

1a Bayford St, E8 3SE
www.facing-heaven.com
Insta: @facingheaven
Travel: London Fields LO
Tue-Thur 18:00-22:00, Fri-Sat 18:00-22:30

For almost anyone who's been on the hunt for good vegan cooking in London over the last few years, they'll likely have heard of Mao Chow. This was the much-admired pit stop for Chinese staples like dumplings and their famous dan-dan noodles - a saucy, spicy affair showered in peanuts. Well, the team behind these tastiest of creations has set up shop right around the corner under a new guise, inspired by a type of chilli pepper popular in Sichuanese cuisine. Along with the change in name, they've added a reimagined menu featuring their culinary hallmarks like scallion pancakes and congee, as well as remixed dishes including chilli oil & soy sauce sundaes or cherry coke char siu skewers. Be warned, the food is spicy and the atmosphere racy - it's channelling a dive bar with its chequerboard flooring and neon lighting. The formula is working as this little place off Hackney's Mare Street is packed every evening. Salads, sides and desserts start around £6, whilst mains range between £10 to £12, but we think its best if you take a friend or few, and order as much as you can to share, perhaps over some beers or a bottle of wine (its BYOB).

££
Vegan

STAGRAM:
_grandhowl
FI PASSWORD:
olfofwellstreet
BATCH
HOT CHOCOLATE

The Grand Howl ❺

Coffee and cooking that'll make you howl with pleasure
214 Well Street, E9 6QT
020 3659 9631
www.thegrandhowl.com
Insta: @the_grandhowl
Travel: Homerton LO
Mon-Fri 08:30-16:30, Sat & Sun 09:00-16:00

This neighbourhood café's name is somewhat quizzical when you consider how, tucked away down a lovely residential street, it isn't trying to draw too much attention to itself. Instead, they quietly get on with what they do best, serving great coffee, alongside vegan and vegetarian cooking that might just make you howl with pleasure. Pastries and cakes are as creative or classic as can be, with pistachio pancakes and milk tarts joining blueberry muffins and brownies. Savouries are the sort to make you salivate - think brioche buns stuffed with breadcrumbed aubergine schnitzels or Brazilian bean enchiladas. For the less adventurous they also offer vegan Full English breakfasts and similar café staples. With meals priced between £6 and £9, The Grand Howl blows the local competition out of the water in its value for money, unless you count the chippy (we don't). Plus, it's got that mix of charm and cosiness that makes it an ideal space to relax with brunch or get some work done with a laptop. If you're looking for a relaxed, local café in E9, The Grand Howl is a perfect pit stop.

£
Vegetarian

The Spread Eagle ❻

London's first vegan pub
224 Homerton High Street, E9 6AS
020 8985 0400
www.thespreadeaglelondon.co.uk
Insta: @thespreadeaglelondon
Travel: Homerton LU
Mon-Thur 16:00–23:00, Fri 16:00-01:00,
Sat 12:00-02:00 & Sun 12:00-22:00

Six years after Soho saw the first veggie pub open in the capital at Norman's (now sadly shut), Hackney has welcomed London's first vegan pub with open arms. The Spread Eagle first made its name with a long-term residency with Club Mexicana. Since those early days they've changed a lot and shifted their menu to focus on plant-based British pub grub. Here you'll find your comfort food needs met but with a refreshing lack of faux meats on the menu. Their inventive use of vegetables is to the fore with Sunday roast offerings such as beet wellington, pot roast celeriac and potato crackling, all with a generous serving of roasties, seasonal greens and Yorkshires. While their weekday menu is more international in scope (think Spanish tortilla and mushroom kebab), you'll still find refreshing reinventions of British classics like the pie, mash and liquor. Snacks and sides cost between £4 and £6, and bigger meals between £8 and £18. There are many friendly regulars who have been coming for years, ensuring that you still get a proper pub vibe, despite the polished and trendy interior. The place is family and dog friendly during the day and hosts lively music nights and slightly wilder events like drag shows in the evenings. If this isn't a testament to how veganism can be for everyone then we don't know what is – a must-visit for a vegan good time in east London.

££
Vegan

SOLD HERE
WHOLE
SCOTCH
LOBSTER !

Sutton & Son's Vegan Chip Shop 7

Fish and chips, without the fish
218 Graham Road, E8 1BP
020 3645 1801
www.suttonandsons.co.uk
Insta: @suttonandsonsvegan
Travel: Hackney Central LO
Daily 12:00-22:00

Although this honourable mention does serve actual fish across its three branches, it is still by far among both the best and first places in London where you can indulge in the most iconic of British dishes, but in an all-new vegan format. Forget 'tofish', for banana blossom marinated in seaweed and samphire, is the key ingredient here that gives it the crucially convincing taste and texture. Add to the usual roster of battered fish and chips some other classics like prawn cocktail, calamari, scampi or pie and mash (again, all vegan), and you'll never need to look elsewhere for 'chippy tea' - as it is affectionately known in the North - ever again. What's more, with all their meals costing under £10, this could easily become your new Friday night ritual. With sides and drinks for between a quarter and half the cost of a meal, it needn't break the bank. Should you want to eat in, the atmosphere is friendly and there is plenty of seating.

£
Vegan

Temple of Hackney 8

London's first vegan chicken shop

5 Morning Lane, E9 6NA
www.templeofseitan.co.uk
Insta: @templeofseitan
Travel: Hackney Central LO
Daily 12:00-21:00

Temple of Seitan hardly needs introducing. They took the chicken shop and transformed it into a delicious vegan treat. As pioneers of vegan street food, they enjoyed instant success with long queues for their deep-fried seitan. The hype might have died down, but their following has remained strong and further branches have followed. Seitan, or wheat meat, might sound a bit glutinous for your liking, but the Temple's faux chicken isn't far off the real deal you'd get from KFC. The batter balances crunch against the bite of the 'chicken', creating a texture that's difficult to differentiate from meat. The spicy burger and wrap are equally good here, but the wings with buffalo sauce can be a bit hit and miss. The menu features decent chips, slaw and mac n' cheese too - allowing you to enjoy a substantial and filling meal. The prices are very reasonable - £6 gets you a great burger and just add £2 for chips and a drink. The Hackney outlet is laid out like a typical chicken shop. Regardless, there's no excuse not to ditch your Dixy's and try one of the capital's most popular vegan indulgences.

£
Vegan

Branch at:

Temple of Seitan, 43 Parkway, Camden, NW1 7PN (see p. 95)
419 Coldharbour Lane, Brixton, SW9 8LH (see p.204)

WAVE - We are Vegan Everything ⑨

Minimalist interiors meet maximalist ingredients

11 Dispensary Lane, E8 1FT
07734 253 401
www.weareveganeverything.com
Insta: @wearewaveldn
Travel: Hackney Central LO
Mon-Sat 08:30-17:00, Sun 10:00-16:00

The world would arguably be a better place if more street corners had a WAVE on them. Alas, so far only the Borough of Hackney has any, but between their first and newly opened Stokey site, they serve up the sort of breakfasts and brunches that made Instagram influencers make veganism their identity. And you needn't worry, for the food tastes as good, if not better, than it looks. The most photogenic of pancakes come adorned with caramelised apples, crumble and cream, whilst toasties take things to a new level packed full of tofu, tomatoes and tasty salad. From the far-flung like açai bowls to the familiar like croissants and brownies, are on offer too, to be enjoyed alongside their artisan coffee, teas or shakes. Big all-day brunch dishes cost around the £10 mark, whilst drinks, baked goods and bagels range between £3-£7. The airy and comfortable interior is a perfect place to enjoy an hour or more, so you can wave goodbye to lunchtime meal deals with We Are Vegan Everything.

£-££
Vegan

Hackney Wick

Barkney Wick Café

Not just for dogs

Unit E, The Smoke House, 75 Smeed Rd, Fish Island, E3 2NE
07723 188 312
www.barkneywick.squarespace.com
Insta: @barkneywick
Travel: Hackney Wick LO
Mon-Wed 08:00-14:30, Thur & Fri 08:00-23:00, Sat 10:00-16:00

Adjacent to this popular dog day-care centre is a plant-based café that serves up, amongst other things, Lick & Mix shareable hound and human treats. If puppuccinos and pupcakes aren't your idea of a treat then fear not, for their regular coffee, normal pastries and sweet treats are worth the excursion alone. Look past the dog toys, chews, balls and pampering products, to find vegan goods made by local bakers like savoury croissants, banana bread, cakes, or paninis, as well as coffee by Dark Arts. Not only is this a hub for dogs and their owners, but they also run events like vegan sushi workshops, which are a great way to learn new things whilst meeting like-minded people. All their packaging and takeaway cups and tubs are recycled or biodegradable, and they give away 'Magic Bags' of food via Too Good To Go, the food waste-reduction app – making them both ethical and low waste. The space is attractive, airy and modern, and much more WFH-friendly than you'd expect from a place full of pooches. What's more, the food is all great value, making this place kind on your purse and your pooch.

£
Vegan

Ethical Bean Company

More than just a company
41 Dace Rd, E3 2NG
0737 969 9318
www.ethicalbean.com
Insta: @ethicalbeancompany
Travel: Hackney Wick LO
Daily 07:00-18:00

The first thing you see as you approach this café in the heart of Hackney Wick's very own Fish Island is a façade of street art that visually represents the places where the cafés coffee comes from. Inside, you'll find that this independent family business offers a friendly welcome and serves great vegan and vegetarian food, ranging from falafel wraps to all-day breakfasts, as well as freshly squeezed juices, protein shakes, gluten-free cakes and more. Local tradesmen and hipsters alike can't get enough of the peanut butter blondies, halloumi bagels or platefuls of hash browns, from a menu which is in the owner's own words '95% vegan'. Despite being minutes away from the Olympic Park, Ethical Bean Co. feels hidden away from the hustle and bustle, especially on a pleasant day when you can use their outdoor seating for some people-watching. Bigger dishes like the full veggie breakfast or their burgers cost around £10, whilst smaller ones like sandwiches, sweet treats and sides go for around £5 to £6. It's a reliable place to stop for a veggie snack when exploring Hackney Wick.

£
Vegetarian

SPITALFIELDS, SHOREDITCH & BRICK LANE

1. Alter
2. Bubala
3. Club Mexicana
4. Dark Sugars
5. Dauns
6. Merkamo Ethiopian
7. Oliveira Kitchen
8. Pilpel, Old Spitalfields Market
9. Pilpel, Brushfield St
10. Tofu Vegan
11. Unity Diner
12. Vegan Yes
13. Veggie Pret
14. Vida Bakery
15. The Vurger Co
16. What the Pitta!

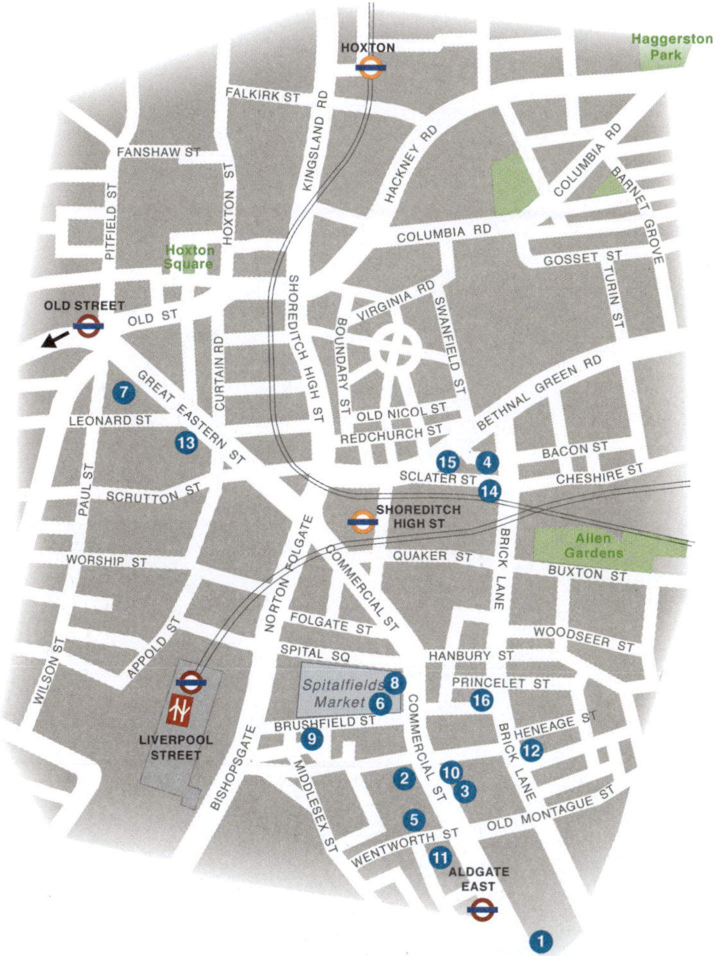

HOXTON
Haggerston Park
FALKIRK ST
KINGSLAND RD
HACKNEY RD
FANSHAW ST
COLUMBIA RD
BARNET GROVE
PITFIELD ST
HOXTON ST
COLUMBIA RD
GOSSET ST
Hoxton Square
TURIN ST
SHOREDITCH HIGH ST
VIRGINIA RD
SWANFIELD ST
OLD STREET
OLD ST
BOUNDARY ST
CURTAIN RD
BETHNAL GREEN RD
GREAT EASTERN ST
LEONARD ST
OLD NICOL ST
REDCHURCH ST
BACON ST
SCLATER ST
CHESHIRE ST
PAUL ST
SCRUTTON ST
SHOREDITCH HIGH ST
BRICK LANE
Allen Gardens
NORTON FOLGATE
COMMERCIAL ST
QUAKER ST
WORSHIP ST
BUXTON ST
FOLGATE ST
WOODSEER ST
APPOLD ST
SPITAL SQ
HANBURY ST
WILSON ST
Spitalfields Market
PRINCELET ST
BRUSHFIELD ST
COMMERCIAL ST
HENEAGE ST
BRICK LANE
LIVERPOOL STREET
BISHOPSGATE
MIDDLESEX ST
OLD MONTAGUE ST
WENTWORTH ST
ALDGATE EAST

Alter 1

Veganism reaches further heights
15 Leman St, E1 8EN
020 3867 7893
www.alterldn.com
Insta: @alter_ldn
Travel: Aldgate East LU
Mon-Sat 12:00-21:00

This self-described vegan izakaya and dive bar would be recognisable to most as a small plates restaurant, and we're not alone in regarding it as one of the best. Serving up pan-Asian cuisine inspired by, amongst other things, the chef's time spent working in the kitchens at some of London's most established restaurants, including Som Saa and A. Wong. Here you'll find plenty of dishes that delightfully riff on street food found across southeast Asia and beyond. Kung-pao crackers reinterpret the classic of local Chinese restaurants, whilst shiitake dumplings, tea leaf sticky rice and laksa, further bolster the menu with big-hitting flavours.

Foodie podcast fans out there will know that comedian James Acaster's favourite bread-based dish, as described in his acclaimed Off Menu show, is the 'pizza' here. The triangular dough balls with an oh-so umami coating are perfect for some dunking in a mouth-wateringly garlicky mess of ajo blanco. If you've ever enjoyed the popular ones from Pizza Express, Alter's version represents its ultimate gastronomic evolution. Situated on the first floor of the Leman Locke Hotel, you get a room with a view thrown in for free. Dishes range between £3 and £13, but most small plates are £6 and larger ones £10. Drinks wise, the cocktails go for £11 and bottles of natural wine start at £33. Unsurprisingly considering its hype, it's important to book in advance.

£££
Vegan

Bubala ❷

Darling of East London's diners

65 Commercial Street, E1 6BD
www.bubala.co.uk
Insta: @bubala_london
Travel: Liverpool Street LU
Mon-Sat 12:00-15:00 & 18:00-23:00, Sun 12:00-16:00

This corner of Shoreditch has been known for Jewish and Middle Eastern food for generations, so it hasn't always been vegetarian-friendly (think Beigel Bake's famous salt beef beigels on Brick Lane). Enter Bubala. Taking its name from the Yiddish for darling, Bubala is winning over more hearts by the day with its Levantine fare. We think Bubala knows best when it comes to exploring dishes from this most fertile of cuisines which we are increasingly familiar with through cookbooks by the likes of Yotam Ottolenghi. Tasting menu or à la carte, either way, you're taken on a tour that traverses confit latkes and labneh, to burnt butter houmous and slices of halloumi that steal the show through their intimate acquaintance with sesame honey. And the interior is as aesthetic as the food, so if you're the Instagram type ensure you've charged your phone – it's all beautiful ceramic tiling around the bar, rustic wooden furnishing, ambient lighting and indoor plants galore. Dishes range between £4 and £14, although almost all cost £7, so take friends and try each and every one of them. And rest assured, there's plenty of natural wine and cocktails to go around too, should that be an essential component of an evening well spent.

Vegetarian
££

Branch:
15 Poland Street, Soho, W1E 8QE (see p.39)

Branch

Club Mexicana 3

46-48 Commercial Street, E1 6LT
www.clubmexicana.com
Full review see p.43

Dark Sugars 4

Chocolatier

Dark Sugars Chocolates, 141 Brick Lane, E1 6SB
Dark Sugars Cocoa House, 124-126 Brick Lane, E1 6RU
www.darksugars.co.uk
Insta: @darksugars
Travel: Shoreditch High Street LO/Liverpool Street LU
Open: Daily 10:00-22:00

Dark Sugars have two branches on Brick Lane. Both outlets boast a ridiculous variety of both vegan and dairy-based chocolate truffles. We can't get enough of their vegan stem ginger chocolates, but whether it's popping candy, sea-salt caramel pearls or chocolate and rum liqueurs that you're after, just follow the sweet scent of cocoa on any visit to Brick Lane. Prices are based on weight in-store or fixed rates for online sales, but the quality of these handcrafted chocolates is worth every penny. Particularly recommended are Dark Sugars' 'signature boxes'.

££
Vegetarian
Gluten-free

Dauns 5

A new dawn for Scandinavian cuisine
77 Wentworth St, London E1 7TD
0748 153 5768
www.dauns.co.uk
Insta: @dauns_scandifood
Travel: Aldgate LU
Tue-Thur 09:00-19:00, Fri & Sat 10:00-20:00, Sun 10:00-16:00

Scandinavian food means a few things to most people – principally smørrebrød, the open sandwiches that usually feature a smoked or pickled fish atop of rye, perhaps under a sprinkling of dill. You might also be familiar with the highs and lows of hallowed food institutions like Noma and Ikea (if you know about the vegan meatballs, you know). You'll find that all at Dauns, but made plant-based, as well as some wild cards like quesadillas and toasties (the latter of which are my personal favourite, owing to their use of great, locally made, nut-cheese). Or else Saturday brunches and Sunday roasts, which forgo bacon for seitan, and focus on the best bits – the trimmings. If you just want something light to go with your morning coffee, then this is the place to choose too, for their daily rotation of Danish pastries is worth its weight in gold – you can never go wrong with a kanelbullen (cinnamon bun). As to be expected with the Scandis, the space is impeccably designed – light, airy and full of foliage atop modern wooden furnishing. Main meals cost between £12 to £15, whilst toasties are half as much, and baked goods half as much again, so you won't be out of pocket if Dauns looks too good to pass by (and it is).

££
Vegan

Green Plate

Merkamo Ethiopian ❻

The soul of East Africa in the heart of East London

Old Spitalfields Market, Horner Square, E1 6EW
www.oldspitalfieldsmarket.com
Insta: @merkamo.ethiopian
Travel: Liverpool Street LU
Mon-Sat 11:30-17:00, Sun 9:00-17:00

Merkamo Ethiopian is the latest eatery on the block bringing East African cuisine to East London. Their success may be in no small part down to their making injera - the flatbread central to the region's cooking - more inviting as bite-sized rolls (rather than a large piece eaten with the hands). You'll find it hidden amongst the sumptuous vegetable stews and salads that sustain the Tewahedo tradition of faithful abstinence from animal products characteristic of East African culture. Ingredients like lentils, spinach, okra and sorghum take pride of place in dahls and curries - this food is as healthy as can be - and is perhaps best washed down with an authentic Ethiopian spice tea. With almost all their large bowls under £10, you'll eat very well here on a budget. Merkamo occupies a unit within the market and shares the covered seating with all the other eateries here, so be prepared to wait for a space when things are busy or to eat shoulder-to-shoulder with other diners.

£
Vegan

Oliveira Kitchen 7

Brazil meets Britain in this modern veggie bistro

80 Paul Street, EC2A 4NE
020 7729 0481
www.oliveira.kitchen
Insta: @oliveira.kitchen
Travel: Old Street LU
Tue & Wed 18:00-23:00, Thur-Sat 12:00-14:30 & 18:00-23:00

Oliveira Kitchen is playing the long game in winning over punters to a plant-based diet. Rejecting faux meat, all dishes are conjured up using only what nature has to offer. In its place they serve some of the best vegetarian food you'll find in the capital, think less "it tastes just like beef" and more "how have I never tried beefsteak mushrooms before". Their Amazonian head chef's intimate knowledge of the diversity of ingredients to be found from far-flung places means dishes are as daring as 'forest floor calamari' made from wild Kaong seeds, cupuaçu mousses or jabuticaba sorbets, as well as quality British produce, such as Kentish sea buckthorn caviar and wild-foraged truffles. This is artistic cooking to pique your curiosity, whilst being approachable in its adoption of comforting classics. Starters and desserts hover around the £10 mark, whilst mains range between £20 and £25. New and old-world natural wines start at £28 a bottle. Oliveira's interior manages to be chic and modern without being overbearing, which describes the whole experience of dining there, making it an essential visit for anyone in London looking to eat well with a lighter ethical footprint.

£££
Vegetarian

Branch

Pilpel 8
Old Spitalfields Market,
Unit E, Pavillion Building, E1 6EW

Pilpel 9
38 Brushfield Street, Spitalfields, E1 6AT
www.pilpel.co.uk
Full review see p.30

Branch

Tofu Vegan 10
54 Commercial Street, Spitalfields, E1 6LT
www.tofuvegan.com
Full review see p.132

Unity Diner ⓫

Ethical eatery by Earthling Ed
60 Wentworth Street, E1 7AL
www.unitydiner.co.uk
Insta: @unitydiner
Travel: Liverpool Street LU
Tue-Thur 12:00-22:00, Fri & Sat 12:00-23:00

Ever heard of Earthling Ed? The long-haired vegan educator and YouTuber has cropped up on ITV's infamous This Morning debates more than a few times defending veganism. His cool-headedness in these discussions has culminated with his Penguin-published book 'This Is Vegan Propaganda'. But you might not know he also co-founded a vegan restaurant in late 2018, as part of his campaign to change public perceptions about plant-based food. Unity Diner dishes up reliable vegan junk food like tofish, chicken wings, burgers, loaded chips and waffles. What makes this restaurant really stand out is its 'unity' with vegan brands. For while the expansiveness of the menu may raise eyebrows, you needn't worry because each of the products is nation-leading in its niche, be it Dappa's mouth-watering vegan nut ice cream or Tindle's 'made with chefs, for chefs' chikn. With the slogan 'the future is vegan' adorning the wall, the Unity Diner certainly wears its heart on its sleeve - there's even a vegan dog menu. The food is priced firmly in the mid-range, with mains around the £15 mark, and sides, desserts and drinks starting at half of that.

££
Vegan

Vegan Yes
VEGAN
YES

Vegan Yes ⓬

Italian Korean fusion
64 Brick Lane, E1 6RF
www.veganyes.uk
Insta: @vegan_yes
Travel: Shoreditch High Street LO/ Liverpool Street LU
Daily 11:30-21:00

Not the usual vegan fare, but one that works all the same - Vegan Yes serves Italian and Korean fusion cuisine from its tiny restaurant on Brick Lane. Food ranges from pasta dishes like lasagne, gnocchi and zuppa, to Korean wraps, salads and sushi-like dishes called gimbap, most of which are loaded up with kimchi. The majority of the dishes are a mix of the two cuisines which makes for an interesting culinary experience. They also serve a good choice of drinks, both alcoholic and soft, as well as a couple of dessert dishes like chocolate-coated rice balls called mochi. Their street food offering is homemade, with 'large' pasta dishes costing between £10 and £15. Vegan Yes's Korean cum Italian food is an unusual fusion, but one that has survived the lockdown and remains one of the most unusual vegan eateries in London and one well worth trying.

££
Vegan

Branch

Veggie Pret ⓭

Veggie only sandwich shop
www.pret.co.uk
57 Great Eastern Street, EC2A 3QD
For review see p.57

Vida Bakery ⓮

Gluten-free vegan cake
139 Brick Lane, E1 6SB
www.vidabakery.co.uk
Insta: @vidabakery
Wed-Fri 12:00-17:00, Sat 11:30-18:00, Sun 11:00-17:00

Vane and Dani have been providing delicious vegan and gluten-free sweet treats at markets and events for a while, but their cute little shop only arrived on Brick Lane in the summer of 2018. Having a place of their own has brought out Vida's aesthetic instincts with a smart moss-green shop front and clean white interior, made more welcoming with comfy cushioned benches and a changing display of artwork.

The cupcakes come in a range of flavours including Oreo, double chocolate and lemon cheesecake, and are all freshly baked and taste as delicious as they look. If the display of cupcakes doesn't take your fancy they also have a choice of cakes, brownies and cookies from which to choose - including their signature Rainbow Cake. Vida also serves great coffee and soft drinks to accompany your guilt-free, sweet treat. Brick Lane can get a little hectic at times and Vida offers a welcome calm space in which to relax and watch the world go by beyond its large glass shop front. Dani and Vane have not entirely settled down and still find time to set up at occasional vegan markets, as well as baking vegan cakes to order - three-tiered Oreo wedding cake anyone?

£
Vegan
Gluten-free

VIDA Bakery

The Vurger Co

The Vurger Co 15

Every option imaginable

Unit 9, Richmix, Avant Garde, Cygnet Street, E1 6LD
www.thevurgerco.com
Insta: @thevurgerco
Travel: Shoreditch High Street LO/Liverpool Street LU
Daily 12:00-21:00

This on-trend burger joint is doing everything right as far as vegan eating goes. It's located among Rich Mix's cultural complex, which includes a popular cinema and events space and is just a few minutes stroll from Brick Lane. The Vurger Co makes healthy, plant-based patties that really hit the spot. And they have succeeded in becoming London's favourite (or at least most hyped) vegan burger. They've done this with their signature brioche buns absolutely stacked to the brim. All this is matched with a huge amount of choice, with seitan chicken, a BeyondMeat burger and veggie-rich and plant-based options (like their Auburger), all on the menu. Even with the often under-considered fry you can choose between tater tots, 50/50 fries, sweet potato fries or skin-on. The shakes and desserts are also well worth a try. The prices are competitive so it's all thumbs up for the Vurger Co.

£-££
Vegan

Branch

What the Pitta! 16

London's first vegan kebab shop

53 Brick Lane, E1 6PU
www.whatthepitta.com
Full review see p.99

Walthamstow

Bühler + Co

Walthamstow neighbourhood café
8 Chingford Road, E17 4PJ
020 8527 3652
www.buhlerandco.com
Insta: @buhler_and_co
Travel: Walthamstow Central LU
Mon & Tue 09:00–15:00, Wed-Sun 09:00–15:30

The residents of Walthamstow are lucky to have such a good café tucked away within their suburban streets. In the light-filled and minimal interior, Bühler + Co serves vegetarian and vegan café staples but with gourmet ingredients and presentation. Their French toast is a real treat, they make a mean veggie fry-up and do a range of quirky cakes including unusual ingredients like quinoa. They also offer dinner service on certain evenings, featuring creative bowls inspired by Asian cuisine, with our favourites being laksa, dumplings with plum sauce and the especially aesthetic bao buns.

The prices are a bit more than you'd usually expect to pay in the area, with substantial dishes costing at least £8, but then again this isn't any old café. They also source a lot of their produce from some of the best regional suppliers, like Climpson and Sons coffee and Chegworth Valley juices. Bühler + Co host regular events in their large space, including exhibitions by local artists. Walthamstow might be a distance for many to travel, but Bühler + Co is well worth seeking out.

££
Vegetarian

Branch

Bodega 50

Homemade café staples

442 Hoe Street, E17 9AH

Insta: @bodega50

Full review see p.140

DALSTON'S
CHICKENish

Chickenish/The Green Grill

Two names, one kitchen
23, Crate Building, 35 St James Street E17 7FY
0794 3806 893
www.chickenish.com / www.thegreengrill.com
Insta: @chickenish / @thegreengrill
Travel: St James Street LO
Mon-Wed 17:00-21:30, Thur 12:00-21:30,
Fri-Sat 12:00-22:00, Sun 12:00-21:30

Serving from the same shipping container, Chickenish and The Green Grill set themselves apart from other purveyors of the meaty, rather than leafy, kind of vegan cooking. Their fried chicken, burgers, hot dogs and ice cream all lack any animal products, but also they deliberately use soy meat rather than seitan. This not only makes the food gluten-free (whereas seitan is literally wheat cake), and therefore available to anyone with such intolerances, but also makes it high in protein, although we wouldn't suggest it's a health-food. Still, that's not really what you think about when you're after some fried food to dunk in a pot of gravy, truffle mayo or buffalo sauce. The menu is minimal, for burgers you can choose between the 'Mighty Meaty', which mixes the classic tomato, lettuce and gherkin with their less traditional charcoal bun, and their 'Green Monster' which has a patty made of peas, broccoli, spinach, peppers and sun-dried tomato beneath a pickled red cabbage dressing. Korean fusion hot dogs see the wiener disguised with kimchi. Dappa - the holy grail of vegan ice cream brands - is the dessert of choice. Combo meals cost around £12 making this an enjoyable way to ethically indulge in some dirty vegan delights.

££
Vegan
Gluten-free

The Gleaners Café (@ the Hornbeam Centre)

Pay-what-you-feel community café

458 Hoe Street, E17 9AH
020 8558 6880
www.hornbeam.org.uk/gleaners-café
Insta: @the_gleaners_cafe
Travel: Leyton Midland Road LO / Walthamstow Central LU
Thur-Sat 11:00-15:00

As the march of gentrification in East London spreads wider and wider, more people are priced out of the 'luxuries' of a decent cup of coffee and a warming meal. Enter Gleaners, a wonderful café making a difference through its pay-what-you-feel policy. Located within the Hornbeam Centre, it is open to everyone and was conceived as a space that truly serves the community. Not only this, but all the delicious food on offer is made using surplus produce that would otherwise go to waste.

Upon entering the café, patrons can choose from four payment scales, based on their ability to pay. The first scale, which is the most economical, charges £1 for a full lunch and 25p for a tea, while the most costly category charges £10 for a full lunch and £2.50 for a tea. Or, those that can't afford the lowest option are also welcome to eat for free. The food they offer is well worth the highest pay grade, with a menu that changes daily and remains seasonal. On any given day they might offer kimchi congee, falafel burgers, dahl, chargrilled padron peppers or miso tofu noodle soup. It's the very best of home-cooking and never gets boring. The café is a real gem with a loyal following among locals and one well worth going out of your way to visit.

£
Vegan

Shri Lakshmi Foods

Hindu cooking from Hyderabad
82 Hoe St, E17 4PG
020 8257 3351
www.shrilakshmifoods.co.uk
Insta: @shrilakshmifoods
Travel: Walthamstow Central LU
Mon-Sat 17:30-22:00, Sun 17:00-21:00

Anglo-Indian cooking often conjures images of chunks of chicken floating in a pool of korma sauce, but as you may be aware, authentic Indian cuisine is one of the few that is often naturally vegan or vegetarian. This is in large part owing to the country's 80% Hindu population and their abstaining from beef because of the cow's holy status. Shri Lakshmi's founder Nihar Baldev takes this a step further by making his menu even more inclusive - it's gluten-free and there's plenty on offer for those with nut allergies too. Instead, ingredients like tamarind and bhel puri (puffed rice) take pride of place, enjoyed best either from their leafy terrace or at home via their tiffin box service. Shri Lakshmi's menu offers moreish starters like chaat and kachori (deep-fried pastry stuffed with lentils, green peas and spice), to vada pav AKA the Bombay Burger (Indian chip butty made famous by Dishoom) and dahi vada - dumplings made from mung beans and lentils, all served with delicious chutneys and yoghurt. Big bowls of curry cost around £12, whereas starters, snacks and sides range from £3 to £7, making this a great place for a veggie Indian feast.

££
Vegetarian

Spicebox

Reimagined Indian in East London

58 Hoe Street, E17 4PG
020 8521 0906
www.eatspicebox.co.uk
Insta: @eatspicebox
Travel: Walthamstow Central LU
Tue-Sun 17:30-21:30, Sat & Sun 11:00-14:00

Spicebox founder Grace's love for Indian cuisine and culture was fostered by her Great Aunt Dolly and further developed during her travels to India. After ditching the day job in Silicon Valley, she decided to pursue her true passion and opened a takeout business with her curries drawing crowds at many of London's food markets. Eventually, she realised the dream of opening her own curry house, with the help of business partner Alpesh. The result is one of the most colourful restaurants in the coolest of East London's neighbourhoods - Walthamstow.

It is here that you can enjoy vegan korma, vindaloo and dhansak classics with bhajis and samosas. Perhaps the best of these Anglo-Indian adaptations is 'The Full Indian' featuring spicy jackfruit beans, crispy Bombay hash, 'Symplicity sausage', Indian guacamole, pickled pink onions, chutney, roasted mushroom and toasted sourdough. Dishes range around £8 to £12, whilst mainstay drinks like lassis and Cobra beers are between £4 and £7, so it's by no means one of the cheaper curries in town, but definitely one of the best. If you leave already thinking of your next Spicebox fix, check out their Tiffin Club where you can pay a one-off £12.50 fee and reuse the steal tiered tiffin for every takeaway order.

£-££
Vegan

PLANE

Shops & Services

Central

Alara Health Store

Vegetarian food store and deli
58-60 Marchmont Street, WC1N 1AB
020 7837 1172
www.wellnatural.co.uk
Insta: @alarahealthshop
Travel: Russell Square LU
Mon-Fri 09:00-19:00, Sat 10:00-17:00, Sun 10:00-16:00

One of the first eateries to cater for vegetarians in central London, Alara now survives amid a plethora of vegan and veggie restaurants around King's Cross. Functioning primarily as a vegetarian health foods store, it stocks a range of products like herbal remedies, pre-packaged sandwiches and dairy-free milks. They also have a pay-by-weight buffet service selling dishes such as stuffed aubergines and leafy salads, which are popular with both regulars and passersby. Bear in mind, however, if buying food from here you are limited to sitting outdoors or taking your food away.

The store offers an extensive and carefully chosen range of skincare including the brands Ren and Green People as well as a choice of cruelty-free cosmetics from the likes of Dr Hauschka. Alara has a great atmosphere, reasonably priced groceries and health food products and is a good choice for a buffet meal on fine days.

££
Vegetarian

Neal's Yard Remedies

Established name for ethical shopping
15 Neal's Yard, WC2H 9DP
020 7379 7222
www.nealsyardremedies.com
Insta: @nyr_official
Travel: Covent Garden LU
Mon-Sat 10:00-20:00, Sun 11:00-18:30

Neal's Yard Remedies is a household name and for good reason. It has been producing natural organic health and beauty products for decades, ranging from skincare to aromatherapy to supplements. They even stock diffusers and books on healing foods. All their products are certified cruelty-free and recognised by major ethical trade markers like Fairtrade and PETA. Their shops also offer therapy rooms where you can get facials as well as homeopathic consultations and courses covering acupuncture, nutritional workshops and more. Neal's Yard Remedies is a unique independent store and one that should be firmly in the minds of health-conscious vegans.

Branches at:

Westfield Stratford City, Ground Floor, Montfichet Road, E20 1EL
Islington, 295 Upper Street, N1 2TU
Borough Market, 4 Stoney Street, SE1 9AA
Unit 51, St Pancras International Station, N1C 4QP

EDEN

West

Eden Perfumes

Perfume for plant-based people
203 Portobello Road, W11 1LU
020 7792 5551
www.edenperfumes.co.uk
Travel: Ladbroke Grove LU
Mon-Sat 10:00-18:00, Sun 11:00-17:00

Originally founded in Brighton, Eden Perfumes is a family-run vegan perfumery that has a smartly fitted-out shop on Portobello Road. Using ingredients derived from vegetable products, they're able to replicate many favourite designer fragrances without any cruelty involved, which is an issue too often ignored by larger name brands.

They also stock aftershaves, colognes and scented candles, meaning there's something for everyone at Eden Perfumes. Their fragrances are very affordable, with prices starting at £18 and going up to £48 for a 50ml bottle, making them far cheaper than the designer equivalent. Eden offers samples and friendly service, so customers can find exactly the perfume that's right for them. They are well worth a visit if you're in Portobello and also have an excellent website from where you can order for home delivery.

GreenBay

Cruelty free supermarket
228 North End Road, W14 9NU
020 7385 8913
www.greenbaysupermarket.co.uk
Travel: West Kensington LU
Mon 13:00-20:00, Tue-Fri 12:00-20:00,
Sat 11:00-20:00, Sun 12:00-18:00

London's first cruelty-free supermarket has joined a plethora of plant-based eateries on North End Road and is just a few doors down from the renowned 222 Vegan Cuisine (see p.153). GreenBay may only be small but it manages to cram in a wide range of groceries, health foods and cosmetics with over a thousand products in its physical store and plenty more available via its website.

GreenBay goes above and beyond to ensure that its stock avoids animal products and is sourced from eco-friendly and ethical suppliers. Here you'll find fresh groceries, 'cheezes', milks and faux meats. They also offer dry foods like pulses, cereals, sauces and spreads as well as health and beauty products. Prices are slightly above the average, which is understandable considering that they're operating on a much smaller scale. They also stock many obscure and speciality products that will not only make a vegan's life a lot easier but also show omnivores that nowadays everything you need can be plant-based. Though the larger retailers have begun to cater to the growing demand for vegan products, GreenBay still stocks a far more impressive variety of goods. If you can't make it to North End Road, they also offer home delivery via their easy-to-use website.

Planet Organic

The largest wholefood chain in London
23-24 Tottenham Court Road, W1T 1BJ
020 3073 1038
www.planetorganic.com
Travel: Tottenham Court Road LU
Mon-Fri 07:30-21:00, Sat 08:00-21:00, Sun 12:00-18:00

London's largest organic supermarket chain has been in business for over 25 years. In recent years they've expanded and now have stores across the capital. As well as selling their own-brand products, they offer a wealth of goods from various established names that include nutritional supplements, fresh groceries, eco-cleaning and cruelty-free beauty products. In case you're peckish, their stores also have salad bars and many take-away food options, as well as juices and coffee. If you have your own containers, some stores now offer plastic-free dispensaries for everyday goods like nuts and grains. While meat and dairy is sold here, there's a growing emphasis on free-from products. Delivery is available throughout the UK.

Branches:
42 Westbourne Grove, W2 5SH
6 Hampstead High Street, NW3 1PR
30 Broadway Market, E8 4QJ
153 Tower Bridge Road, SE1 3LW
201 Chiswick High Road, W4 2DR
111-17 Muswell Hill Road, N10 3HS
64 Essex Road, N1 8LR
117-21 Salusbury Road, Queen's Park, NW6 6RG
132 Commercial Street, E1 6NG
17-21 High Street, Ealing W5 5DB
186-88 Balham High Road, SW12 9BP

Portobello Wholefoods

Old-school health food store

266 Portobello Road, W10 5TY
020 8968 9133
Travel: Ladbroke Grove LU
Mon-Sat 09:30-18:00, Sun 11:00-17:00

Portobello Wholefoods has been sheltering under the Westway on Portobello Road for decades. It survives by providing great value and friendly service and offering a really wide selection of healthy produce for the denizens of Portobello. They are particularly good for their selection of loose teas, locally sourced fresh bread and vegetables - making this a good place to get the basics. If you need vitamins and supplements they also have a huge variety and helpful staff on hand to offer advice. Portobello Wholefoods is a really old-school establishment (no website or social media) but all the better for that and long may it continue to thrive. If you're in the area and looking for somewhere to eat don't forget Portobello Health Foods (see p.175).

Stella McCartney

Cruelty-free fashion house
23 Old Bond Street, W1S 4PZ
020 7518 3100
www.stellamccartney.com
Insta: @stellamccartney
Travel: Green Park LU
Mon-Sat 10:00-18:30, Sun 12:00-18:00

One of the most prominent fashion brands in Britain, Stella McCartney is also one of the only high-end labels to have a vegetarian ethos. The label does use wool and silk but avoids leather and fur in its designs and offers many specifically vegan-friendly shoes and garments. The company pioneers ethical practices, including the use of synthetic wool and silk alternatives. The label offers Ready-To-Wear ranges primarily for women, with a more limited offering for men and children.

Stella McCartney has downscaled its high-street presence in recent years and now concentrates on its concept store on Old Bond Street in the heart of Mayfair. It's an incredible experience visiting this store, but good things don't come cheap, especially in the fashion world, and this label is very much at the high end of things. A simple t-shirt starts from close to £200 and more elaborate dresses and outerwear sometimes cost upwards of £2000. Stella McCartney does however offer a more affordable line in collaboration with Adidas that is both stylish and sporty. These prices might be out of most people's budget but it's good to know there is a high-end vegetarian fashion label available for those that can afford it.

South

Fareshares

Food co-op and community project
56 Crampton Street, SE17 3AE
www.fareshares.org.uk
Travel: Elephant and Castle LU
Thur 14:00-20:00, Fri 16:00-19:00, Sat 15:00-17:00

Fareshares is a food co-op in south London that has been providing affordable healthy food since the 90s. They stock all sorts of fresh fruit and veg, as well as dry goods like grains, nuts and pulses, all in bulk and as cheap as possible. They also offer bread, bottled goods and great organic produce and are pioneers in zero-packaging. This not-for-profit, community initiative is as good as it gets.

PIPOCA

Zero-waste vegan store and café
224 Brixton Road, SW9 6AH
www.pipocavegan.com
Insta: @pipocavegan
Travel: Brixton LU
Tue-Sat 10:00-20:00, Sun 10:00-17:00

Pipoca began life as a zero-waste store and has since expanded to provide food and a vegan café (see p.202). Almost all your vegan essentials are taken care of, with those extra niceties for when you want to splash out a little. Plant-based frozen pizzas, freshly baked sourdough, craft beers, and artisan nut spreads are just some of the things to reward your visit to this stylish modern store. The café is a good one, so you can enjoy a cheeky snack while shopping for the essentials.

PIPOCA

East

Dark Sugars
Chocolatier

Dark Sugars Chocolates, 141 Brick Lane, E1 6SB
Chocolate Shop, see p.297
Dark Sugars Cocoa House, 124-126 Brick Lane, E1 6RU
Chocolate Café, see p.297

eat17 Hackney
Upmarket wholefood in Homerton
Brooksby's Walk, E9 6DA
www.eat17.co.uk
Insta: @eat17stores
Travel: Hackney Central LO
Mon-Sat 08:00-22:00, Sun 09:00-21:00

Having converted an old cinema into this stylish whole food store, the good people of eat17 have gone from strength to strength offering a fabulous range of organic produce, health foods and fresh goods. They are now a small independent chain and one well worth seeking out. Although selling animal products, veggies and vegans will find plenty to make them smile.

Branches:
24-26 Orford Road, Walthamstow, E17 9NJ
77 Fulham Palace Road, Hammersmith, W6 8JA

Fifth Dimension Tattoo and Piercing

Vegan tattooist and piercing parlour
16 Bacon Street, E1 6LF
www.fifthdimensiontattoo.co.uk
Insta: @fifthdimensiontattoo
Travel: Shoreditch High Street LO/Liverpool Street LU
Mon-Tues (by appointment only),
Wed- Fri 11:00-19:00, Sat 11:00-18:00, Sun 13:00-17:00

Operating as London's only vegan tattoo parlour, Fifth Dimension offers a range of styles from their three in-house artists. They have specialists in geometric and symbol tattoos, as well as new-school art and more classic watercolour work. Full body piercings are also available here and they sell a range of natural aftercare products for both services. Their work can be seen on their website and social media pages, where you can choose among the several resident artists to find the one you like.

Grains & Green

Vegan grocery store
214 Mare Street, E8 3RD
020 8985 6344
Travel: Hackney Central LO
Daily 08:00-21:00

This neighbourhood grocery store is a great option for your weekly vegan goods. It stocks everything from speciality faux meats to cleaning products, as well as whole foods. They're price-competitive to other similar suppliers and also have a small takeout service offering fresh foods like sandwiches. The store is narrow but surprisingly long, with extensive shelving stocking all your vegan needs.

North

Bumblebee Natural Foods

Friendly independent store
33 Brecknock Road, N7 0BT
020 7284 1314
www.bumblebeenaturalfoods.com
Travel: Kentish Town LU
Mon-Sat 09:00-17:30

Bumblebee has been supplying the good folk of N7 with fresh veg, whole foods and dry goods for over 40 years. They operate out of two stores (Veg Shop and Nut Shop) but this unusual arrangement works perfectly. Veggies and vegans will find themselves well catered for and they also offer a veg bag delivery service.

Earth Natural Foods

Grocery as natural as the earth
200-202 Kentish Town Road, NW5 2AE
020 7482 2211
www.earthnaturalfoods.co.uk
Travel: Kentish Town LU
Mon-Sat 08:30-19:00

Earth Natural Foods stocks only organic, vegetarian whole foods and eco-friendly household goods. They stock all the essentials like seasonal fruit and veg, nuts and other dry goods, oils and lots of tempting sweet treats. You'll be able to get fresh sourdough bread, as well as free-from goods and takeaway salads here too. They're also taking a stand against plastic packaging, so bring your own reusable containers and top-up on stock at a discounted rate. They also carry many of the fair trade brands and ethically produced health and beauty products.

Harmless

Vegan, plastic-free and zero-waste store
79 Tottenham Lane, Crouch End, N8 9BE
0737 7322 426
www.harmlessstore.co.uk
Insta: @harmless_store
Travel: Turnpike Lane LU, Hornsey LO
Mon-Thur 10:00-18:00, Sat-Sun 10:00-16:00

Harmless is a vegan business at the forefront of reshaping consumer behaviour for the better. This is a vegan, plastic-free and zero-waste store that sells all the household essentials. Their spread of foodstuffs is extensive, with dry goods like pasta and pulses, dairy-free cheeses, chocolate treats and fresh fruits and veg too. They sell cleaning, health and beauty products and plenty of extras like water bottles and tote bags to help you keep your footprint as small as possible. Their dry goods adorn the walls in big glass containers and you pay by weight. This is a great way for north Londoners to reduce their plastic waste and help the environment – just don't forget to bring your own refillable containers.

The Third Estate

Cruelty free clothing store
27 Brecknock Road, N7 0BT
020 3620 2361
www.thethirdestate.co.uk
Insta: @thethirdestatelondon
Travel: Kentish Town LU
Wed-Fri 10:00-19:00, Sat 10:00-18:00

This clothing retailer operates both online and as an in-store boutique, from where it sells an entire range of casual wear for both men and women, including accessories like belts and bags, footwear and essentials like jackets and jeans. The overall aesthetic of their clothing is British normcore – the style is quiet and suitable for the everyday. You can expect to find a range of speciality vegan fashion lines, as well as some bigger designers like Fred Perry.

With all of their stock The Third Estate ensure their respect for animals is translated into the human world also – only working with suppliers that meet high social, labour and environmental standards. The Camden store is a little off the beaten track on Brecknock Road, but is well worth a visit with great displays and friendly staff who are committed to the principles of cruelty-free living. If all this shopping has left you feeling peckish, the vegan eatery Healthy Wealthy is just opposite (see p.113).

Vegan Supper Clubs

E3 Vegan

Marc Joseph's vegan dining experience
357 Roman Road, E3 5QR
www.e3vegan.com
Insta: @e3.vegan

Marc Joseph made his name at the much-missed Vanilla Black but has since moved onto fresh pastures on Roman Road. For Marc's lovely, everyday cooking visit the café (see p.245), but to experience his full talents book one of the E3 Vegan Supper Club events. The food is remarkable and it's a great opportunity to meet some like-minded diners.

Mav in the Kitchen

Indian supper club
www.eatwith.com
Insta: @mavinthekitchen

Once a month Mav and Julie pull out all the stops for their vegan supper club. The event always takes place at a cosy café near Clapham Junction but the menu changes every time. The dishes may change but the cuisine is always inspired by Mav's Gujurati background fused with western influences. The club is friendly with many regular guests, which is hardly surprising given that it's just £38 per head for a scrumptious three-course meal. To get a better view of what's on offer, check out their Insta feed and get booking!

Right Said Veg

Unique vegan supper club

Salt the Radish, 45 Blackstock Road, N4 2JF
www.rightsaidveg.com
Insta: @rightsaidveg

This incredibly popular vegan supper club has been surprising the taste buds of London's vegan community since 2018. The menu changes with each event but expect to find delicacies like kimchi, sesame and cucumber salad, masala fried cauliflower and shitake, aubergine and black bean stew. The desserts on offer like rhubarb rice pudding are also bound to put a smile on your face. You need to book in advance, but for only £35 per head, the only issue is getting a spot before they've sold out. The club runs regularly and is always based at their Finsbury Park café - Salt the Radish.

Vegan Events

Vegan Nights

Old Truman Brewery, 150 Brick Lane, E1 6QL
www.vegannights.uk
Insta: @vegannightsldn
Travel: Shoreditch High Street LO/Liverpool Street LU
Regular events during the summer months
With the iconic Old Truman Brewery as its venue, Vegan Nights showcases the hottest cooking and entrepreneurship that the plant-based community has to offer. Whether you're after food, vegan products like t-shirts and skin care, or looking to attend a talk or yoga class, they've got you covered. There's lots of vegan fast food on offer and a marquee hosted by DJs such as Melody Kane, so you can make a night of it.

Vegan Life Live London

Alexandra Palace, Alexandra Palace Way, N22 7AY
www.london.veganlifelive.com
Insta: @veganlife_live
Travel: Alexandra Palace Rail, Wood Green LU (then free shuttle bus)
Every February or March
This annual event is a festival of everything vegan with cookery demonstrations, ethical clothing, cruelty-free cosmetics, live performances and Q&A's with experts in plant-based living. Vegan Life is an event where you can spend a day milling around discovering new products and ideas. If you feel peckish there's a food court offering delicious street food, from veggie burgers to substantial Indian curries.

OBEY

Index

Portobello Wholefoods, see p.328

Image Credits

P.II © Punk Pasta, p. 2 Spread Eagle © Jade Nina Sarkhel, p. 3 © Plates, p. 9 ©Flower Burger, p. 16 © Punk Pasta, p. 28 © Pastan, p. 33 © Stem & Glory, p. 38 Bubala Soho © The Food Snobs, p. 40 © Clean Kitchen, p. 42 Club Mexicana © Nic Crilly-Hargrave, p. 44 © Gauthier, p. 48 © Mildred's, p. 64 © The Gate, p. 67 © Plants, p. 68 © Tendril, p. 98 © What the Pitta, p. 103 © Rani, p. 121 © The Gate, p. 131 © Namaste@OMNOM, p. 142 © Made in Hackney, p. 146 © Plant Club, p. 150, Holy Carrot © Joakim Blockstrom, p. 159, Holy Carrot © Joakim Blockstrom, p. 169 ©Clean Kitchen, p. 170 © Farmacy, p. 202 © PIPOCA, p. 228 © naïfs, p. 230 © OMNI, p. 233 © Persepolis, p. 236 © Mallow, p. 241 © Flat Earth Pizzas, p. 267 © Plates, p. 275 © EDIT, p. 282 © Sutton & Son, p. 286 © WAVE, p. 292 Crilly Hargrave © Alter, p. 294 Bubala © Haydon Perrier, p. 299 © Daunsp. 303 © Oliveira Kitchen, p. 313 © **Bühler + Co**, p. 314 © **Chickenish/The Green Grill, p. 319** Spicebox © Justin De Souza, p. 331 © PIPOCA, p.339 © Right Said Veg, p.351 © Mallow.

2nd Edition
"What a great book"
Joe Swift
The
LONDON
GARDEN
BOOK A-Z
Abigail Willis

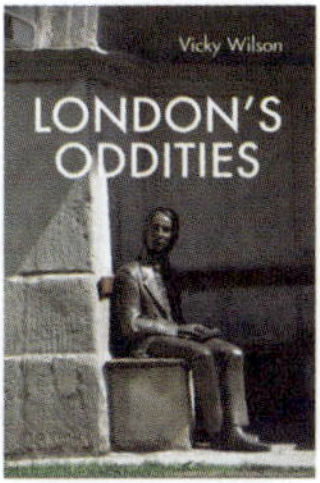
Vicky Wilson
LONDON'S
ODDITIES

LONDON
ARCHITECTURE
MARIANNE BUTLER

ANDREW KERSHMAN
WALKING
CAMBRIDGE
1,000 YEARS OF HISTORY IN 8 WALKS

ANDREW KERSHMAN
WALKING
BRIGHTON
& HOVE

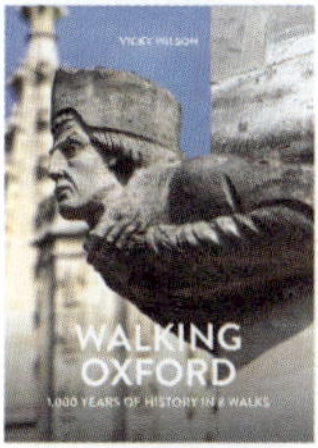
VICKY WILSON
WALKING
OXFORD
1,000 YEARS OF HISTORY IN 8 WALKS

LONDON'S
CEMETERIES
SPEND THE DAY WITH KARL MARX,
ENID BLYTON, KEITH MOON AND MANY MORE

STEPHEN MILLAR
LONDON'S
CITY CHURCHES
FIND THE SCORCH MARKS OF THE GREAT FIRE
OR VISIT AN ALTAR BY HENRY MOORE

EDINBURGH'S
HIDDEN WALKS
WALK, EXPLORE,
DISCOVER...

LONDON'S
HOUSES
FROM WORKHOUSE
TO ROYAL PALACE,
COME IN, CLOSE THE
DOOR AND STEP
BACK IN TIME...

LONDON'S
MONUMENTS
FROM BOUDICCA
AND BYRON TO
GUY THE
GORILLA

LONDON'S PARKS
AND GARDENS
COVER MORE
THAN TWENTY-FIVE
PERCENT OF THE
CAPITAL – THAT'S
A LOT MORE GRASS
BETWEEN TOES
THAN ANY OTHER
CITY IN EUROPE

BROS
V DAWGZ
JAKE'S VEGAN STEAKS
VEGAN

VEGGIE & VEGAN LONDON

Written by Edward Prendeville
Photographs by Andrew Kershman
Cover Photograph: Bubala © Haydon Perrior
Illustrations by Lesley Gilmour and Hannah Kershman
Book design by Susi Koch and Lesley Gilmour
Edited by Eve Kershman

Published in 2023 by
Metro Publications Ltd
www.metropublications.com

Metro® is a registered trade mark of Associated Newspapers Limited. The METRO mark is under licence from Associated Newspapers Limited.

Printed and bound in China. This book is produced using paper from registered sustainable and managed sources.

British Library Cataloguing in Publication Data.
A catalogue record for this book is available from the British Library.

ISBN: 978-1-902910-73-4

FSC
www.fsc.org
MIX
Paper | Supporting responsible forestry
FSC® C016973